GETTING

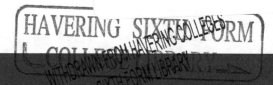

Spelling

CATHERINE HILTON

MARGARET HYDER

46584

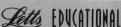
Letts EDUCATIONAL

First published 1992
Reprinted 1993, 1995

Editorial team
Rachel Grant, Andrew Thraves, Angela Royal

Design team
Frank Greenyer, Jonathan Barnard
Text © Catherine Hilton and Margaret Hyder 1992

© BPP (Letts Educational) Ltd
Aldine House, Aldine Place, 142-144 Uxbridge Road, London W12 8AW

British Library Cataloguing in Publication Data

Hilton, Catherine
    Spelling. – (Getting to grips)
    I. Title II. Hyder, Margaret III. Series
    428.1

ISBN 1 85758 091 5

Printed in England by Livesey Ltd., Shrewsbury.

Acknowledgements

Every effort has been made to trace all copyright holders but, if any have been inadvertently overlooked, the publishers will gladly receive information enabling them to rectify any error or omission in subsequent editions.

Pages 9-10, 64 and 69, from *Pocket Oxford Dictionary* (7th edition, 1984), Oxford University Press; pages 29, 68 and 69, from *Chambers Concise Dictionary* (W & R Chambers, Edinburgh 1988); page 31, six bars of *Jailhouse Rock* used by kind permission of Carlin Music Corporation, Iron Bridge House, 3 Bridge Approach, London, NW1 8BD; page 58, from *The Pan Spelling Dictionary,* Pan Macmillan Ltd; page 60, from *The Pergamon Dictionary of Perfect Spelling,* SRA Ltd.

Contents

How to Use this Book 5

How to Use this Book

We hope this book will make you more confident in your ability to spell by

▶ showing techniques that you can use to improve your spelling,

▶ giving background information about the English language,

▶ demonstrating useful spelling rules,

▶ providing examples of 'problem' words and

▶ giving guidance on possible and probable spelling patterns.

SECTION 1 introduces spelling, explains why English spelling can cause difficulties, gives general advice and helps you to understand the philosophy behind this book.

SECTION 2 shows various techniques for improving spelling and how to use them. Some of these techniques are developed further in Section 3.

SECTION 3 helps to consolidate and expand the first two sections by presenting spelling rules and sound patterns.

It is advisable to work through the sections systematically as they build upon one another. However, it may often be necessary to go back to previous chapters to refresh your memory.

As you complete the tasks, check your answers in the answer section. Answers are not given for tasks where you are asked to check definitions in the dictionary or when you are asked to identify parts of words which present difficulties for you. Obviously the latter depends on your individual needs.

Throughout the text, where a new term has been introduced, a short explanation is given. For a fuller explanation refer to **Understanding the Terms**.

1
Why Spelling Is Difficult

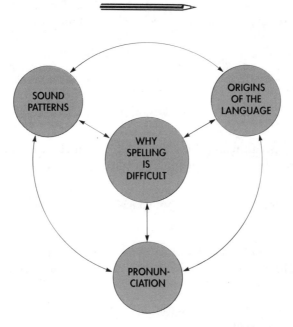

Pronunciation

If all English words were spelt as they are pronounced, people would experience fewer problems with spelling. In some languages the spelling of words exactly reflects the way the words are pronounced. Unfortunately this is not always the case in the English language.

spelt as pronounced	not spelt as pronounced
farm	what
remember	when
limit	month
letter	said
depend	earth
understand	business

As you can see, it is not always the long words that present difficulties: many short, frequently used words are not spelt as they are pronounced. Obviously, trying to spell every word as it sounds ends in disaster.

Individual pronunciation patterns can affect spelling.

This pronunciation problem is further complicated by the fact that in Britain there are many different regional accents. Pronunciation also varies from one English-speaking country to another. The most obvious examples occur with words like 'bath' and 'castle'. In southern English the beginning of these words are pronounced like 'bar' and 'car', but further north the 'ar' sound disappears.

Sound patterns

In the English alphabet there are 26 letters which have to represent approximately 44 different sound patterns (phonemes).

All English words have to be composed from these sounds. If each phoneme were represented by one letter, it would make spelling much easier.

e.g. cloud.

The 'ouch' sound in 'cloud' is made by the letters 'ou' but this same 'ouch' sound can be made by 'ow' in words like 'clown'. Having different ways of spelling the same sound creates problems for spellers.

There are many other examples of different sets of letters combining to make the same sound.

e.g. pursue and perfect

Although both of these words start with the same sound, they are spelt differently.

An individual letter in the alphabet can also be called upon to make more than one sound.

e.g.   yes   fly   happy

In each of these words 'y' makes a different sound.

e.g.

hop	hope
In this word 'o' is a short vowel sound (ŏ). The same sound appears in **rob**, **cloth** and **lock**.	Here 'o' is a long vowel sound (ō). The same sound appears in **code**, **smoke** and **broke**. The 'e' at the end of the word is not sounded but it changes the 'o' to an 'ō' sound.

In Section 3 sound patterns are dealt with more fully. It helps your spelling if you know and understand the sound patterns in English and realise both what is possible and what is probable in a given situation.

Origins of the language

English is part of the group of languages known as Indo–European languages. Old English developed from the Germanic part of this group of languages.

Finding out about the origins of words

These entries form part of a page from *The Pocket Oxford Dictionary* and show the variety of origins of English words.

a′lder (aw′l-) *n.* Tree related to birch (**black**, **red**, **white**, ~, other trees not related). [E] ———————— English
a′lderman (aw′l-) *n.* (pl. **-men**). (esp. Hist.) Co-opted member of English county or borough council, next below Mayor, ~ǐc (-mă′-) *a.*; ~ship *n.* [E (OLD, MAN)]
A′lderney (aw′l-) *a. & n.* (Animal) of breed of cattle from *Alderney* or elsewhere in Channel Islands. [place]
āle *n.* (arch., exc. as trade wd). Beer. [E] ———————— English

English ————

a′leatory *a.* Depending on chance; involving performer's random choice. [L (*alea* DIE¹)]

Latin ————————

alě′mbǐc *n.* Apparatus formerly used in distilling (also fig. *the alembic of fancy* etc.). [F f. L f. Arab. f. Gk *ambix -ikos* cap of still] ———— French from Latin from Arabic from Greek

alẽr′t *a., n., & v.* 1. *a.* Watchful, vigilant; nimble. 2. *n.* Alarm-call; (period of) air-raid warning; **on the** ~, on the look-out. 3. *v.t.* Make alert, warn. [F f. It. *all' erta* to the watch-tower] ———— French from Italian

Aléxa′ndrian (ălǐgzah′-) *a.* Relating to the Hellenistic civilization of *Alexandria* in Egypt, 3rd–2nd c. B.C. [place]

ălĕxă′ndrīne (-īgz-) *a.* & *n.* (Verse) of six iambic feet. [F (*Alexandre* Alexander the Great)]

ălfă′lfa *n.* Lucerne. [Sp. f. Arab., ————Spanish from Arabic = a green fodder]

ălfrĕ′scō *adv.* & *a.* In the open air. [It., = in the fresh (air)]

Italian

ă′lg|a *n.* (*pl.* ~ae *pr.* -jē, -gē). Primitive cryptogram, e.g. plankton, some seaweeds; ~al *a.* [L] ————————————Latin

ă′lgĕbr|a *n.* Investigation of properties of numbers, using letters etc. as general symbols; ~ă′ĭc(al) *adjs.* (-ically); ~(ā)ĭst *ns.* [It., Sp.,—— Italian, Spanish, Latin L f. Arab., = reunion of broken parts]   from Arabic

ă′lgorĭthm (-dhem) *n.* Process or rules for (esp. machine) calculation

French from Latin etc. [F f. L f. Pers. (name of 9th-c. *from Persian* mathematician)]

ă′lĭas *adv.* & *n.* (Name by which one is or was) called on other *Latin* occasions. [L, = at another time]

ă′lĭbī *n.* Plea that when alleged act took place one was elsewhere; (colloq.) excuse. [L, = elsewhere] ————————————Latin

Try selecting a page from a dictionary at random to see if you can find any different word origins. (It may be necessary to refer to the list of abbreviations near the front of the dictionary.)

Difficult spelling patterns

Some words incorporated into our language have been anglicised; others have retained spelling features from the original language.

EXAMPLES:

restaurant (French)

chaos (Greek)

anorak (an Eskimo word)

The following list demonstrates the interesting variety of words we have adopted from other languages. Some of these may present you with difficulties when you come to spell them because of their unusual constructions.

Old Norse/ Scandinavian	French	Latin	Indian	Italian	Spanish
scold	parliament	genius	bungalow	pizza	potato
husband	garage	circle	jodhpurs	replica	patio
skirt	ballet	consensus	shampoo	studio	hurricane
scare	blouse	index	juggernaut	balcony	parade

The path of the English language

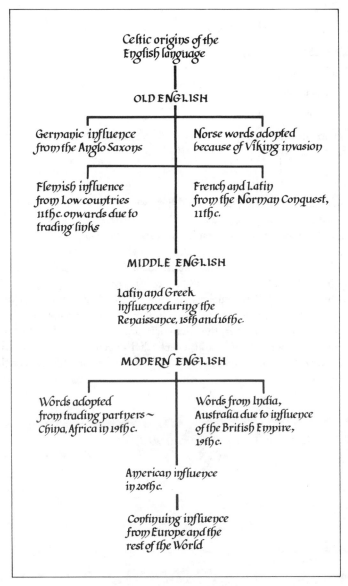

Celtic origins of the
English language

OLD ENGLISH

Germanic influence
from the Anglo Saxons

Norse words adopted
because of Viking invasion

Flemish influence
from Low countries
11th c. onwards due to
trading links

French and Latin
from the Norman Conquest,
11th c.

MIDDLE ENGLISH

Latin and Greek
influence during the
Renaissance, 15th and 16th c.

MODERN ENGLISH

Words adopted
from trading partners ~
China, Africa in 19th c.

Words from India,
Australia due to influence
of the British Empire,
19th c.

American influence
in 20th c.

Continuing influence
from Europe and the
rest of the World

Modern English is a living language which has evolved from a number of other languages and continues to grow and change with time.

The silent letter 'catch'

Another problem encountered by today's writers of English is the number of letters in words that are no longer pronounced so creating **the silent letter 'catch'**.

In Old English all the letters in a word were pronounced.

EXAMPLES:

'k' in knife and knee

'b' in climb and comb

'l' in should and would

The pronunciation of such words changed but the spelling remained the same.

The spelling convention

For many centuries in England people spelt words the way they wished and even chose several ways of spelling a word in the same piece of writing. Although there were periods when English spelling was relatively stable and various attempts were made to standardise spelling, it was not really until Samuel Johnson's dictionary was published in 1755 that spelling patterns became fixed. Dr Johnson wasn't always consistent in his dictionary and is responsible for some of the curious spelling patterns that cause difficulties for today's spellers; for example, he included a 'p' in 'receipt' but not in 'conceit' or 'deceit'. However, this dictionary and its successors did provide a reference so that people could check their spelling. **Once spelling became standardised the ability to spell according to convention became important.**

2

You Can Improve Your Spelling

Some people seem to be natural spellers, others find problems with certain words, whilst many people see themselves as being hopeless spellers. If you were poor at spelling at school, then you may, as an adult, have tried to avoid writing whenever possible. Any skill grows rusty if it is neglected and spelling is no exception.

To improve your spelling you must

see the need

be determined you can improve

work hard at the learning process.

It is not something that will come overnight and no one can wave a magic wand and make you into a good speller. The hard work has to come from you but if you adopt a systematic approach and don't become disheartened, you can be successful. Above all, you must believe in yourself.

Have confidence in yourself
Check your work
Select priority words to learn
How can you improve your spelling?
Develop an interest in words
Plentiful, regular practice
Learn techniques
Know about the language

Have confidence in yourself

Spelling is really a matter of confidence. For fluent spellers, or people who see themselves as not having a problem with spelling, the words seem to be at their fingertips, flowing out of their pens without effort. They rarely stop to think about how to spell a word. For others, spelling is a problem. Many people see themselves as poor spellers. Their assessment of themselves is not always accurate but by having a poor self image, their confidence is diminished. For them, writing means frequent pauses while they search for alternative words when they are uncertain of the spelling of the words they really want to use. They frequently use a dictionary to check spellings. Often the words they check are correct but they lack confidence in their own judgement.

Confidence can come from knowing how to tackle a spelling problem, by constantly practising techniques and by writing as much as possible. If you avoid writing or only select the words you know you can spell, your spelling will fail to improve.

When you feel more positive about spelling, you make fewer mistakes and by making fewer mistakes your confidence increases. Being a poor speller is certainly not all in the mind – it is a real problem but if you give yourself the label 'poor speller' then you will perform according to your label. Instead, tell yourself that although you are not perfect and have some problems with spelling, you are working on them and with determination and practice you will improve.

Remember, there are no perfect spellers but you can improve with practice.

Select priority words to learn

Once you have seen the need to improve your spelling, you have to decide where to start. You will need to identify the words that you frequently want to use and don't know how to spell. These are your **target words** which you will note down in your word book. More advice about word books is given in Section 2. Concentrate on these target words first and leave the words you use less often until later. These can be learnt when you feel more confident about spelling.

Plentiful, regular practice

Spelling is an active skill and to improve you will need to practise.

Practice should involve not only tackling problem words but also trying to find as many reasons for writing as possible. Don't phone, write. The more you write, the more you will find out about the words that constantly present problems for you. Then you can set about dealing with these problem words. Words may need to be practised many times before they become firmly established in your memory.

Practising spelling and writing is like exercising. It is more valuable to have frequent, short practices than less frequent but longer practices. Try to establish a routine so that you set aside a certain time for practising. Perhaps you could keep a diary so that you have a reason for writing each day. Each entry could be very short but include interesting or unusual events, conversations overheard, items from the news or amusing incidents. This way you will need to use a variety of words which will give you as much varied practice as possible. If you only write about your daily routine, you will keep using the same words and won't challenge yourself or use and need to spell a range of words. In addition, make a list of words which present problems and learn a few of these each day.

It often helps to join an English or spelling class at your local college or adult education centre. Such classes are usually very informal and relaxed so you do not have to feel embarrassed about having a problem with spelling. You can share your problems with others who know how you feel and you will also get regular spelling practice.

By repeatedly using problem words in your writing, you will familiarise yourself with their spelling patterns.

Know about the language

As you work through this book, you will learn more about the English language and this will enable you to gain a better understanding of spelling patterns and rules. Such knowledge will not only make learning to spell more interesting, it will also help to increase your confidence in your ability to tackle problem words. In many instances you will no longer have to guess the spellings of words: knowledge of the possible and probable spelling alternatives will help you to make informed choices.

Knowledge of the structure of the English language can help your spelling.

Learn techniques

Learning any skill involves learning about the subject and then finding ways to help you remember this knowledge and put it into practice. If spelling presents problems, you will need to learn techniques which will aid the learning process. Such techniques will help you to remember the individual pattern of each word or group of words.

Different words often require different techniques and some people find certain approaches more helpful than others so you can choose the most appropriate method for a given situation from the variety of techniques presented in this book.

Develop an interest in words

You may have a few problems with spelling but be very interested in reading. People often say that if you read widely, you should be able to spell but this is not always true. Fluent readers read quickly, their eyes moving rapidly across the page, not dwelling upon the individual formation of each word. To remember the spelling pattern of a word, you need to look at it for longer than you do when reading, in order to learn the pattern and commit it to memory.

This does not mean that reading won't help your spelling. Reading introduces you to new words, phrases and ideas which you may use in your writing. It helps to enlarge your vocabulary and shows you the versatility and scope of the English language and we hope it will make you more interested in words.

By being alive to words, you will find it easier to learn to spell.

Check your work

When writing, it is sensible to prepare a rough draft whenever possible. This takes the pressure off you so you don't feel that you have to produce a perfect copy at the first attempt. You can then check this rough draft thoroughly before producing the final copy.

In the rough draft, if you are uncertain of the spelling of a word then write it down as you think it may be spelt. If there is a word that you feel you cannot even begin to attempt to spell, leave a space as you will be able to recall the missing word from its context when you read through the draft. Always complete the entire piece of writing before using your dictionary. If you check each suspect word in a dictionary as you write, you will lose the flow of your writing and lose confidence in your spelling. Once you check one word, you may doubt your judgement on another word and so on until the act of writing becomes laborious and you have convinced yourself you cannot spell.

We all make mistakes when we write. Our brains seem to move ahead of our pens and we don't always write down what we intend. Always proof-read your writing. Try to read it as if it were written by someone else – you will be more likely to spot mistakes. Read slowly as it is easy to read what you meant to write rather than what you have actually written. It may be helpful to carry out more than one check. First read what you have written to see that it makes sense and is punctuated correctly, then look at words individually and concentrate on their spellings. If a word looks wrong, underline it in pencil. Try to spell it in alternative ways to see if one of these ways looks right. After this, check in your dictionary.

Make it a rule to check everything you write.

Guidance

<u>Do</u>	<u>Don't</u>
Do believe you can improve your spelling.	Don't see yourself as a hopeless speller but as a person who has some spelling problems.
Do check everything you write.	Don't think that a problem with spelling stops you being able to write.

Do	Don't
Do practise regularly.	Don't feel embarrassed by not being able to spell words. We all find some words difficult to spell.
Do set aside a short time each day to learn problem words.	Don't despair.
Do take an interest in words.	Don't write in capital letters – fluent handwriting aids fluent spelling.
Do buy yourself a good dictionary.	Don't overuse a dictionary. Always attempt to write a word before you look it up.
Do keep a personal word book or dictionary.	Don't check the spelling of every word as you write. Write first and then use your dictionary at the end.
Do use a spell check on a word processor if you have one.	
Do select target words to learn.	

Helpful Hints

Before going on to Section 2, pause and think about your own spelling. It may be useful to write down your thoughts.

Why do you want to improve your spelling?

Why is spelling difficult for you?

What types of mistake do you make?

How do you try to remember problem words?

How much time do you plan to set aside for practising?

What opportunities do you have for writing?

What other writing opportunities could you devise?

Think positively and adopt a strategy towards improving your spelling.

3
Looking at Words

Spelling is primarily a visual skill

Good spellers write confidently, automatically spelling words correctly because they can 'see' the words in their minds and transfer the picture correctly to the page. They have a good visual memory, although they may not necessarily be aware of this skill, and appear to recall words effortlessly.

Ways of developing your visual memory

If you find it difficult to 'take a picture' of a word and remember the shape so that you can produce it correctly whenever you need it, you can actively improve your visual memory.

▶ Train yourself to become more observant.

▶ Become more aware of words and their appearance.

▶ Read widely and regularly.

▶ Look for words when you watch television.

Train yourself to become more observant

You can improve and develop your visual memory as you go about your everyday life. Training can take place at any time or anywhere and can help to pass the time while you are standing at bus stops or travelling on trains, buses, etc. Look at people, cars, houses and advertisements. Study them carefully then close your eyes and try to visualise the person or object in detail.

Whenever you see a collection of objects, look at them closely, noting the position of each and its distinctive features. Then close your eyes and try to create the same image in your mind.

By concentrating on details, actively memorising them and then trying to recall them, you will gradually improve your visual memory.

Become more aware of words and their appearances

Look carefully at the overall shape of words.

Note the characteristics of the word shapes which distinguish one word's appearance from another. In 'struggle' your eyes may be drawn to the 'gg', the 't' and the 'l'. You are noticing the special features which give 'struggle' its distinctive shape.

Obviously some words are visually similar, so you may need to find different techniques for these words.

** Look at the overall shape of these words and decide on their distinctive features.

diary	nobody	fly
office	goldfish	church
bedroom	newspaper	telephoning
pyramid	joyful	disappoint

Helpful Hints

It is important to use lower case letters when you are writing a word you wish to learn, as by writing in capitals you lose the individual shape of the word.

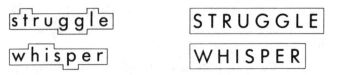

You will also find it easier to spell words correctly if you adopt a cursive style of handwriting. If you write each letter individually without joining it to the next, you interrupt the flow of the word and the sequence of the letters.

plinth   *nephew*

Remember, when copying a word from the dictionary, to check that you have spelt it correctly. Careful copying and careful writing will help you to learn the word more easily.

Read widely and regularly

In Chapter 2 it was pointed out that reading does not necessarily influence people's spelling ability. However, the more often you see a word in print, the more familiar you will become with its shape and pattern. The likelihood of your retaining its picture and so spelling it correctly is increased.

You probably read for many purposes and will not always wish to spend too long on the individual appearance of a word. But it is helpful, particularly when reading technical or other unfamiliar material, to focus your attention on the appearance of any unfamiliar words, so establishing the overall shape in your memory.

Look for words when you watch television

Television is a powerful visual medium of communication, and advertisers in particular recognise the importance of the visual memory. Words and slogans are often flashed on to the screen to be imprinted in the viewer's memory. Not all of the words will be useful to you but by actively looking at words that appear on the screen and attempting to memorise them, you will develop your visual skills.

The visual technique

This technique for remembering the spelling of words is especially useful for difficult, irregular words. This technique can be summarised

Look

Cover

Write

Check

The visual technique

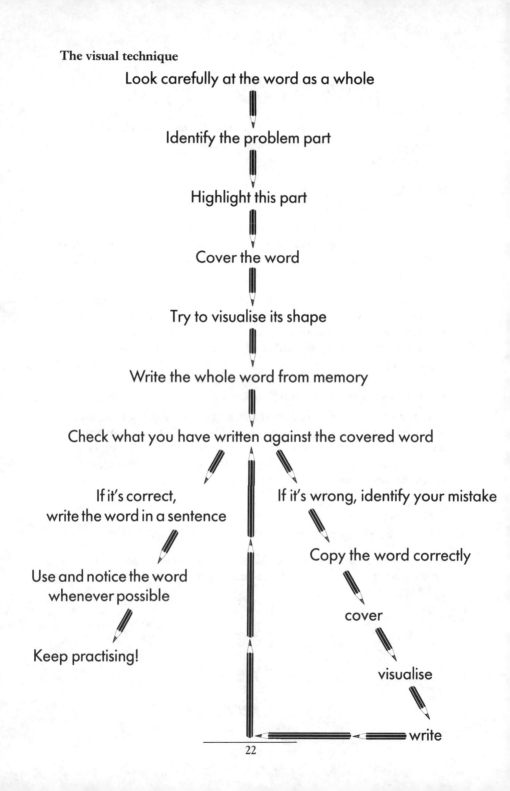

Look carefully at the word as a whole

Identify the problem part

Highlight this part

Cover the word

Try to visualise its shape

Write the whole word from memory

Check what you have written against the covered word

If it's correct,
write the word in a sentence

Use and notice the word
whenever possible

Keep practising!

If it's wrong, identify your mistake

Copy the word correctly

cover

visualise

write

**Try using this technique with these words which can present difficulties.

amateur	dialogue	saucer
gauge	colour	sausages
surprise	among	moustache
shoe	analysis	anxious
patient	attach	said

Combining techniques

The learning of words visually may be combined with other techniques.

Mnemonics

If you find it difficult to remember a particular feature of a word visually, you may be able to use the problem letters to create a picture which will help you to recall the letter order.

e.g. awkward

People often have difficulty with the letters 'wkw'. Imagine an awkward school boy whose name is William K. Williams. He is very clumsy, frequently trips over and is always in the way. Whenever you wish to write the word 'awkward', connect the image of this boy with his name, William K. Williams, and recall the 'wkw' pattern in 'awkward'.

Tracing

You may find tracing words with your finger helps to reinforce the visual aspect of words. The movement of the finger helps to fix the pattern of the letters. If you say each part as you trace the word, this will act as further reinforcement.

Every time you practise the word, using the **look, cover, write, check** method, first trace the word out on paper to recall the 'feel' of it before you actually write it. This may seem a rather lengthy process but it has proved to be effective for some people and is ideal for words which give you special problems.

Why use the visual technique?

▶ Sight is the sense we rely upon most and is our most developed sense. As it is so important to us, using our visual sense is probably the most effective way of improving our spelling.

- Learning the spelling of a word by the visual technique can work for every word. Indeed for some words no other technique can be applied.
- Research has shown that about 30% of words that adults write can't be spelt merely by listening to the sound pattern.

The hidden 'catch'

This occurs when letters are silent or when letters appear in an unusual combination.

e.g. daughter

This word sounds as if it should be spelt 'dorter'. The speller has to remember the look of the word and focus on the 'augh' part in order to spell it correctly.

** Identify the 'catch' in each of these words. Focus your attention on it and then test yourself by covering up the word and writing it down. You may find some words need extra practice.

thorough	eighth	environment
fascinate	imaginary	carriage
gradual	especially	rhythm
answer	schedule	vacuum

Phonic alternatives

Sometimes there is a number of alternative ways of spelling a sound.

e.g. ē may be made by 'ea' as in **meat** or 'ee' as in **feet** or 'e–e' as in **complete**.

In such instances, the speller will probably make the correct choice by remembering the word visually and knowing which alternative looks right.

** Choose the correct spelling from these pairs of words.

conceel/conceal	poyson/poison
announce/annownce	valew/value
desine/design	pairent/parent
scandle/scandal	drowsy/drousy
fourty/forty	receed/recede
proceedure/procedure	rehearse/reherse

Practising

You can use the **look, cover, write, check** technique to test and practise spellings.

At school you may have practised spellings by writing out words three, five, or even ten times. This isn't particularly helpful as it allows you to adopt a passive role and encourages inaccurate copying and careless writing.

A more useful approach is to write out the word in full; on each line below write the word again with successive letters missing, then write the complete word again at the end.

e.g.

February

ebruary

F bruary

Fe ruary

Feb uary

Febr ary

Febru ry

Februa y

Februar

February

It sounds tedious but it works! You're concentrating on the individual letters in the word *and* on the word as a whole.

** Missing letter exercises are very useful in helping you to build up a picture of a word and remember the letters in the right order. Test yourself with the following words.

sug_ _stion	str_ _ght	thor_ _gh
nece_ _ary	ob_y	expe_ _ence
oc_ _sion	b_ _lding	enthu_ _astic
re_l_y	suc_ _ed	mu_ _le

pu_ _tual	dis_ _tisfy	pe_ _le
T_ _sday	b_a_tiful	la_ _hter
mes_ _ge	an_ _ous	hei_ _t
c_p_ble	altho_ _h	e_ _ly
li_ _son	ba_ _elor	ad_ _cent

Writing tricky words on cards can be helpful. Leave the cards in a prominent place so that you are often reminded of how the words look. It works best if the card is white and the word written on it is in bold, black letters.

These cards can be stuck on the front or back of cupboard doors at eye level. Direct your eyes to each card several times during the day; look at the word; look away or close your eyes and try to visualise the word, retaining the picture in your mind's eye for several seconds.

The more frequently you practise, the easier it will be to remember the shape and spelling of a word. If there is a particular part of a word that presents difficulty, try, when visualising it, to 'pin' those letters securely to the card.

Some computer games can help with spelling. The type of spelling program which displays a word on the VDU screen, asks you to study it, clears the screen and then invites you to type in the correct spelling, has proved to be very effective. If you make a mistake, the correct version is shown and you can try again. Such programs usually have a facility for you to enter words in the memory so you can practise them.

Proof-reading

If you are uncertain of the spelling of a word you have written, you will probably write it out in various ways to see which version looks right and then choose the spelling that appears correct. By training yourself to look at words more actively and carefully, you will increase your chances of seeing which words have been misspelt. You will also increase your knowledge of probable letter combinations.

** Practise your proof-reading ability by identifying and correcting the spelling errors in this letter.

```
                                        High School

                                        Glenview Road

                                        Blankton

                                        Greyshire

                                        14 February 1992

   Mr A. Johnson

   36 Stone Lane

   Blankton

   Greyshire


   Dear Mr Johnson,

              I am sory to have to imform you that your

   son, John, has been late for school on three occassions

   resently.

              He used to be a very hard working,

   concientous young man but, since Christmas, he has been

   most unrelyable and akward.

              I would be greatfull if you could make an

   apointment to see me so that we can disscuss

   his behavour. Tuesday is the most convinient day for me.

   My secretry will make all the neccesary arrangments.

              I look foreward to meeting you.

              Yours sincerley,


                     Bob Pritchard
```

** Use the visual technique to decide which word of each pair is correctly spelt.

suppose/supose	suceed/succeed	pritty/pretty
verry/very	many/meny	ownly/only
oringe/orange	signe/sign	juise/juice
biscuit/biscit	groupe/group	queu/queue
mouldy/moldy	doubble/double	sience/science
weather/wheather	disapoint/disappoint	through/thourgh

As you can see, the ability to remember the visual image of a word is a valuable skill. It is worth working on even if at the moment you don't have a very good visual memory. However, if you have great difficulties and seem to make no progress, don't despair. There are other techniques you can use and, as Chapter 2 pointed out, once you know several techniques then you can choose the one that suits you and is most appropriate for the word you are trying to learn.

4
Taking Words Apart

The visual aspect of spelling is extremely important and you need to train yourself to notice the pattern of a word and focus on the unusual or difficult parts. In Chapter 3 you practised looking at whole words in order to remember their spelling patterns. That technique is especially valuable for words which you use frequently or words that have difficult or irregular patterns.

In this chapter you will be introduced to a spelling technique which you can use alongside the visual technique. **Here you will be concentrating on parts of words, a piece at a time, rather than the word as a whole.** This is called dividing a word into syllables or **syllabification**.

What is a syllable?

This is the definition of a syllable in *Chambers Concise Dictionary*.

> **syllable** sil'a-bl, n. a word or part of a word uttered by a single effort of the voice.
> **syllabifica'tion** pronunciation as a syllable: division into syllables.

In **Understanding the Terms** we define a syllable as 'a word or part of a word that can be made by one effort of breath'.

Recognising syllables

Words can be **monosyllabic, disyllabic** or **polysyllabic**.

A monosyllabic word contains one syllable.

EXAMPLES:

ache	bear
word	strength
force	pair

If you say these words aloud, you will need one effort of breath to pronounce each word.

A disyllabic word has two syllables.

EXAMPLES:

bot/tom	hus/band
nev/er	af/fect
tab/let	chap/ter

Two efforts of breath will be needed when you say these words.

A polysyllabic word will have three or more syllables in it.

EXAMPLES:

con/tin/ent	hap/pin/ess
dis/or/der/ly	ex/tra/or/din/ary
pho/to/graph/ic/al/ly	un/con/stit/u/tion/al/ly

Many people avoid writing long words as they find them difficult to spell but if words are divided into syllables, you can see they are made up of shorter, more familiar parts.

Helpful Hints

If the idea of syllables is new to you, then it may help if you cup your hand firmly under your chin while you say the following word clearly and loudly:

fantastic.

You will feel your chin pressing into your hand three times, once for every syllable.

** You may like to try out these words in a similar way.

1 pronunciation

2 ice

3 remember

4 butter

5 disconnecting

Check your results in the answer section.

In singing it is difficult to sing a long word, made up of several syllables, to a single note of music so usually there is a note for each syllable.

Jailhouse Rock

Words and Music by Jerry Leiber, Mike Stoller

1. The war- den threw a par - ty in the coun - ty jail.___ The
2. Spi - der Mur-phy play'd the ten - or sax - o - phone. __

pri - son band was there and they be- gan to wail.___ The band was jump-in' and the joint be -
Lit - tle Joe was blow - in' on the slide trom-bone. __ The drum-mer boy from Il - li -nois went

If you have problems with dividing words into syllables, you could always try putting the words to music!

Guidelines for dividing words

▶ Just as every word in English contains a vowel so does every syllable, but you have to remember that 'y' can also be a vowel at times. For example, in 'hap/py', the 'y' sounds like an $\bar{e}$; in 're/ply', the 'y' sounds like an $\bar{\imath}$.

▶ A syllable can also be a vowel on its own.

e.g. o/pen

▶ If two identical consonants appear together in a word then it is best to divide between these consonants.

EXAMPLES:

let/ter	run/ner	kip/per	bet/ter
stag/ger	rum/mage	ter/ror	ap/point

This draws your attention to the two consonants and helps you spell the word correctly. If you pronounce each syllable as you write the word, then you will hear the two consonants.

e.g. ap/point

You hear the 'p' at the end of the first syllable and the 'p' at the beginning of the second syllable.

▶ Although there are other rules for dividing words into syllables, dealt with in Chapter 9, it is better to follow your own personal preferences and divide words in ways that are most helpful to you.

Practising the technique

** You may like to try dividing these words into syllables so that you get used to spotting individual syllables within words. You can check the answer section afterwards.

reinforce	forgotten
drawing	cardigan
rehabilitation	occupy
absolute	unfit
orbit	supervise

Why is this technique useful?

▶ It makes long words less daunting to spell.

▶ It helps with words you are not accustomed to spelling.

▶ It allows you to break words into more manageable units.

▶ It enables you to concentrate on one part of a word at a time and notice its pattern.

▶ It helps you to become more aware of the sounds of the language.

▶ It makes you realise how words are built up.

▶ It forces you to look more closely and carefully at a word.

▶ It encourages you to be more analytical about words.

▶ It stops you omitting a syllable from long words.

▶ It helps you to see short words within longer words.

▶ It draws your attention to patterns within families of words.

▶ It is particularly helpful if it is used in conjunction with adapted pronunciation (see Chapter 5).

Words within words

In this list each word has been divided into syllables. Where the syllable forms a word in its own right, it has been printed in colour to draw your attention to it.

to/mor/row	hope/less/ness
es/tim/ate	bar/bar/i/an
be/gin/ning	gar/den/er
main/ten/ance	en/close
cut/ler/y	chim/pan/zee

You will notice that some syllables are not pronounced in the same way in the short word as they are in the complete word.

e.g. bar/bar/i/an

The first 'bar' sounds exactly like the short word 'bar':

The second 'bar' sounds more like 'bear'.

The 'i' sounds like the vowel sound ē.

Your attention will be drawn to this again in Chapter 5 when you consider adapting the pronunciation to accord with the way the word is spelt. However, even without adapting the pronunciation, **the ability to see a word within another word helps to jog your memory.**

** Try underlining the word or words within each of these words.

suppose	defrost
climate	average
acquaintance	blessing
frightened	ordinary
disgusting	pigeon

Sometimes you will see words within words that do not conform to the division of the word into syllables. For example, 'sin/cere/ly' divides into three syllables. Without the division, you can see since and rely. Knowing that **since** and **rely** go together to make up **sincerely** is very useful when it comes to remembering how to spell it.

'hol/id/ay' can be divided into three syllables but without the division, you can see lid in holiday. Being able to see this could stop you misspelling **holiday**.

Compound words

Often, separate words are put together in English to form a longer word. **It helps when spelling if you can identify the separate words within the longer word.**

EXAMPLES:

kid	+	nap	kidnap
head	+	quarters	headquarters
farm	+	house	farmhouse
read	+	able	readable

down	+	ward	downward
tar	+	get	target
wind	+	mill	windmill
wood	+	worm	woodworm
bed	+	room	bedroom
French	+	man	Frenchman

** You may like to pair off the words from the two columns below. One has been done for you.

bird	thing
snow	sticks
any	stairs
over	fruit
chop	cage
card	ball
down	board
grape	room
cloak	storm
thunder	lap

Reviewing syllables

** Complete each word by filling in the missing syllable.

crim........   un........stand

af........noon   blan........

pic........   ....bey

be........ning   mush........

in........esting   pros........ous

Dividing words into syllables will not help you to spell every word you have difficulty with as English is not a phonetically regular language. You have already seen in the word 'bar/bar/i/an' that all the syllables do not sound the same as they are spelt.

When you sound out a syllable, you may find you have chosen the wrong combination of letters to represent the sound.

e.g. fer/til/i/ser

fer	til	i	ser

Here the 'er' sound is made by 'er' but you could have incorrectly chosen 'ir' or 'ur' as in other words these combinations of letters are used to make the same sound.

In fertiliser 'til' has one 'l' but you could have chosen to put 'll' to match 'till' when it appears in its own right.

You could have begun this syllable with a 'z'. This would have been quite correct as it can be spelt either 'ise' or 'ize'.

Syllabification works best with words that are spelt as they sound, for example 'splen/did' and 'per/haps'. In some words you can mispronounce a syllable so that it fits the spelling pattern (see Chapter 5) but for other words you will need different techniques.

Syllabification is a helpful technique if you allow it to take its place alongside other spelling techniques. By the end of this book you will be able to decide which technique is suitable for a particular word. Its major advantage is that it draws your attention to the construction of words and makes you look at their individual parts.

EXAMPLES:

an/al/y/sing — 'y' makes an $\bar{\imath}$ sound; the word ends in 'sing'.

fact/u/al — Syllabification draws attention to the 'u' and stops you missing it out.

li/ bra /ry — Your eye is drawn to the well-known abbreviated word 'bra' and so you remember the 'r' after 'b'. It is a common mistake to leave it out.

veg/e/ta/tion	Here the 'e' is highlighted so you can't forget to write it down.
e/con/o/my	It is helpful to divide this word in a different way, e/co/no/my, then you can see the pattern 'co' 'no'. You can also see 'my' at the end.
be/lieve	In the second syllable you can see the word 'lie'. It's not a **lie**, I be**lie**ve it!
ac/cid/ent	Perhaps the CID will investigate this accident!

These are all personal observations but you can make up your own for words which cause you trouble.

** Select a page from a newspaper or magazine and copy down any words that may give you difficulty if you were to try to spell them. Concentrate on those that can usefully be divided into syllables and then work on the different syllables and see if you can devise your own memory aids. Your ingenuity and creativity may surprise you!

5
Adapting the Pronunciation

In Chapter 4 you practised dividing words into syllables so that you could concentrate on the spelling of the individual parts of a word. This is a useful technique if the syllables of the word are spelt as they are pronounced.

EXAMPLES:

lad/der	ad/mit	fin/ger	yes/ter/day	re/fer
im/por/ter	en/joy/ment	prop/er/ty	cred/it	hap/pen/ing

Knowing the sounds

▶ Single consonant sounds

▶ Consonant blends

▶ Consonant digraphs

▶ Vowel sounds

5

In order to be successful at spelling each syllable it is necessary to understand the sounds that the individual letters of the alphabet make and the sounds associated with a group of letters.

You will find it useful to read this section on sounds thoroughly now, and then to use it as a reference section as you work through the other parts of this book.

It is easier to deal with the consonants in the alphabet first. Each of these has a name but the sound each makes is different from its name. If you say each word aloud in a clear voice, it will help you appreciate the sound each consonant makes.

Single consonant sounds

b	boy	cab
c	can	act
d	dear	adapt
f	fish	often
g	goat	again

h	hand	inhabit
j	jar	rejoice
k	kettle	woke
l	leg	almost
m	man	arm
n	no	men
p	penny	ape
q	quarter	equip ('q' is always followed by 'u')
r	rabbit	hero
s	sad	crease
t	tank	tent
v	vegetable	have
w	window	unworthy
x	box	axe
y	young	beyond
z	zoo	lazy

'w' only has its consonant sound at the beginnings of words or after a prefix. (In the word 'unworthy', 'un' is a prefix.) Elsewhere 'w' combines with other vowels to form a vowel sound, e.g. 'aw', 'ew', 'ow'.

'y' has its consonant sound at the beginning of a word. In other places it has the long vowel sounds $\bar{e}$ or $\bar{\imath}$.

EXAMPLES:

pretty ($\bar{e}$)

supply ($\bar{\imath}$)

Consonant blends

When certain consonants appear together they blend into one another. Each letter retains its separate sound but the sounds slide together. If you can recognise these blends it will help you to spell the beginnings of certain words.

You will notice that two or three consonants can blend their sounds together. Again you will need to say each word slowly and clearly so that you can hear the blend.

bl	blue	blot
br	brush	bright
cl	club	clue
cr	crowd	creature
dr	dress	drink
fl	flag	fling
fr	front	frill
gl	glad	glamour
gr	ground	grow
pl	place	plane
pr	present	property
sc	scope	scale
scr	scrabble	screw
sk	skate	skin
sl	slam	slink
sm	small	smack
sn	snow	snack
sp	spin	spider
spl	splutter	splendid
spr	spring	sprint
squ	squeeze	squirrel
st	start	stuck
str	strong	string
sw	swing	switch
thr	three	thread
tr	tree	trick
tw	twig	twelve

** Beside each blend write down another word beginning with the blend. If you cannot think of a word for a particular blend, use your dictionary.

Consonant digraphs

When these consonants appear together, their sounds do not blend – the letters go together to produce one sound instead.

sh	shine	shock	push
ch	change	choice	much
th	then	there	that
	thin	thick	pith

You will notice that the 'th' sound in the first row of 'th' words has a slightly different sound from those in the second row.

wh	whip	while	white
ph	photograph	phantom	phone

Notice that all these combinations of letters contain an 'h'.

** Use the consonant digraphs above to complete these words. Say the words aloud as you write them to ensure that you have chosen exactly the same sound as made by the pairs of consonants in the words above.

_ _urch	_ _easant
_ _isper	_ _irst
_ _isky	lur_ _
hu_ _	pa_ _
_ _ake	paragra_ _

Vowel sounds

Vowels are more difficult because they can each have more than one sound. These sounds are called short or long sounds. The pronunciation of vowels also differs according to accent.

Short vowel sounds

When you say these words aloud, you will hear the sound associated with the letters a, e, i, o, u.

a	apple	cat
e	egg	pet
i	ink	pin
o	oblong	top
u	umpire	mug

Long vowel sounds

Here the vowels have the same sounds as the names of their letters in the alphabet. As you say these words aloud you will hear the alphabet names a, e, i, o, u.

a	ate	brave
e	eve	compete
i	drive	idea
o	open	spoken
u	unit	fuse

In dictionaries, vowels are marked with either a *breve* (ˇ) above them for a short vowel sound, or a *macron* (¯) above them for a long vowel sound. This information helps you to pronounce words correctly. The same symbols are used throughout this book.

** Decide whether the vowel sound underlined in each of these words is short or long. Say the word aloud so that you can hear the sound.

defuse	dentist	pupil	acorn
collect	doctor	stake	silent
beware	pistol	saddle	torpedo
hungry	total	hiker	tube
mistake	cabbage	trifle	puppy

Exaggerating the pronunciation

"If only words were spelt as we say them!" is a familiar cry. A great many words are but some are not and many of the latter cause confusion when it comes to spelling. **We cannot change our spelling to fit the pronunciation but we can alter our pronunciation to fit the spelling** of a word. Many people find this a useful technique. It is summarised in the diagram on page 42, overleaf.

Beginnings

In English the emphasis is often put on the first syllable of a word.

EXAMPLES:

dentist	lucid
hundred	diary

Beginnings

Changing pronunciation after 'w'

Endings

Exaggerating the pronunciation

Silent letters

Missing syllables

Parts of words

Words within words

But beginnings of words can present problems, especially if the stress does not fall on this part of the word. Exaggerating the pronunciation of the beginning of the word as you attempt to spell it can be useful.

EXAMPLES:

description	despair
democracy	deposit
despite	design
decision	protrude
precise	production

Endings

The ending of a word is often difficult to spell because its sound cannot be heard clearly. When the stress is on the first part of the word, the voice trails off at the end of the word.

EXAMPLES:

amiable	order
hinder	accent

If you stress the pronunciation of the end of such words when you say them, spelling them becomes easier. When you become accustomed to certain groups of letters appearing at the ends of words you will not need to use this technique as much, as you will begin to appreciate the various patterns and know what is possible and probable.

Some problem endings

The ending 'ed' is never pronounced 'ed'. There are three possible sounds which the letters 'ed' make at the end of a word:

'id'   as in 'posted',

'd'   as in 'killed' and

't'   as in 'dashed'.

If you have problems with 'ed' endings, pronounce the last two letters as 'ed' to rhyme with 'ted' as you write them.

For each of the endings below, read the words in the list aloud and pronounce the ending as it is spelt.

ar	age	ary
particular	passage	contemporary
spectacular	image	primary
grammar	garage	temporary
burglar	village	dictionary
beggar	average	anniversary

ance	ate	al
attendance	chocolate	medical
balance	obstinate	personal
reassurance	separate	scandal
insurance	desperate	sandal
maintenance	accurate	petal

ace	able	ery
palace	agreeable	mystery
grimace	suitable	brewery
surface	charitable	machinery
disgrace	noticeable	crockery
furnace	inflatable	mastery

<u>ain</u>	<u>ant</u>	<u>ence</u>
curtain	elegant	independence
fountain	extravagant	reference
captain	relevant	correspondence
mountain	elephant	existence
certain	defiant	difference

<u>ent</u>	<u>ice</u>	<u>ible</u>
dependent	notice	visible
frequent	novice	impossible
advent	police	edible
convenient	malice	intelligible
imminent	crevice	legible

<u>ory</u>
lavatory
category
factory
oratory
laboratory

It may also help you if you notice that some of the endings form words in their own right.

EXAMPLES:

'age' as in passage

'ate' as in desperate

'able' as in agreeable

'ant' as in elegant

'ice' as in notice

'tory' as in factory

There is more about endings in Chapter 16.

Missing syllables

Some words are misspelt because a part of the word or a letter in it is difficult to hear.

EXAMPLES:

in/ter/est/ing	The 'e' is often missed out.
em/per/or	Again, the 'e' is often omitted.
es/tu/ary	The middle syllable disappears as we say the word.
bois/ter/ous	Stress the 'er' sound.

By pronouncing each syllable slowly and clearly, you can hear the part which is often omitted. **Saying the word as you write it will stop you leaving out letters.**

** Say these words aloud and underline the part that is difficult to hear.

mathematics	vegetable
miniature	library
temperature	virtually
sergeant	vacuum
parliament	people
acquire	Arctic
general	monastery

Words within words

If you can see a word within another word and stress the pronunciation of that shorter word, it will help you to spell tricky words. For example, in the word the/or/y you can see the words 'the' and 'or', but when they occur within the word 'theory', 'the' and 'or' lose their individual sounds. It can help your spelling if you recognise and pronounce the words as they would be pronounced individually.

EXAMPLES:

competent (pet)

character (act)

recognise (cog)

orange (ran or range)

nuclear (clear)

The word within each of the words shown below (printed in colour) can be deliberately mispronounced to assist in its spelling.

friend	foreign
acknow/ledge	appearance
balloon	courteous
early	develop

Parts of words

Sometimes you will be able to identify a part of a word which isn't a word in its own right, yet it is a problem for you to spell. Isolate this part and mispronounce it in the same way as if it were a word. In addition, you may find a 'word within a word' to stress as well.

EXAMPLES:

choc/o/late	Stress the ŏ.
	See the word 'late'.
def/in/ite	Stress 'ite'.
	See the word 'in'.
el/e/gant	Stress the ĕ.
con/tem/por/ary	Stress 'por' and 'ary'.
tem/por/ary	
bach/el/or	Stress the 'ch' sound.
	Stress 'el' and 'or'.
fa/vour/ite	See the word 'our'.
	Stress 'ite'.
rel/e/vant	Stress the ē.
	See the word 'ant'.

When you are using this technique, it is a good idea to underline the difficult part or write it in larger letters or use a different colour. This will draw your attention to the part of the word that is a problem for you.

WedNESday

collaborate

immediately

** Work out the difficult parts of these words and decide which you need to stress.

convenient	pretty
benefit	apparatus
probably	enemy

Silent letters

Adapting the pronunciation of words to assist you with their spelling is especially useful in words that have silent letters. Many of the letters which are now silent used to be pronounced, so perhaps by adopting the pronunciation of your predecessors you won't miss out letters when you spell words!

Knowing about the possibility of silent letters also helps when using a dictionary. If you are aware that a certain letter can be silent at the beginning of a word, you will take this into account when you try to find the word in a dictionary.

EXAMPLES:

a	aisle	extraordinary	miniature
b	lamb	subtle	plumber
c	science	scissors	ascent
d	handsome	dredger	budget
e	dispute	bathe	breathe
g	gnarled	campaign	design
h	honour	exhibition	heir
k	knitting	knickers	knuckle
l	salmon	yolk	should
n	autumn	column	solemn
p	raspberry	pneumonia	psychology
t	listen	match	mortgage
u	biscuit	distinguish	guard
w	write	answer	sword

** Underline the silent letters in these words.

doubt	psalm	descend	mistletoe
kitchen	rhyme	condemn	porridge
ghost	knack	while	bristle
gnaw	love	guitar	edge
knee	known	what	wrinkled

Changing pronunciation after 'w'

▶ 'w' is a very complicated letter. It can be silent.

EXAMPLES:

wrangle

wriggle

wrist

▶ A letter which follows it can be silent.

EXAMPLES:

white

whirl

while

▶ This affects many question words.

EXAMPLES:

why?

when?

what?

▶ It can change the sound of the letter or letters that follow it.

EXAMPLES:

 was

watch — Here each 'a' has an ŏ sound.

want

 ward

warm — Here 'ar' is pronounced 'or'.

reward

 word

worse — Here 'or' has an 'er' sound.

worth

▶ Mispronouncing a word in which 'w' has an influence can help you to spell the word.

Using the techniques

You have now become familiar with three techniques.

▶ **The visual approach** which involves 'taking a picture' of a whole word or part of a word.

▶ **Breaking words into syllables** and concentrating on one part of a word at a time.

▶ **Adapting the pronunciation**: adopting a special pronunciation for a tricky spelling.

Not all words lend themselves to a particular approach and sometimes you may need to use more than one approach at a time to tackle a problem word.

** Look at these words and decide which is the most suitable technique, or techniques, to use.

ought	repetition	routine
beautiful	eighth	disease
chestnut	graduate	transfer
impudent	cupboard	hatchet
ninth	water	vehicle
twelfth	language	whose
building	figure	umbrella

If you train yourself to analyse the way words are made up, you can crack the spelling code.

5

6
Knowing the Rules

Are there any rules?

English is often considered to be an illogical language with no rhyme or reason to its spelling. Certainly, as has already been said, many English words are difficult to spell, yet there *are* rules and established patterns within the language. It is estimated that approximately 85% of words are regular in that they follow a pattern or obey a rule. Knowing the rules and appreciating the patterns can make spelling easier to tackle. It can be another valuable weapon in the speller's armoury.

In Section 3, Chapters 9 to 18, the main rules are dealt with in detail. In this chapter you are introduced to the idea of using rules and presented with a number of rules to try out. Use this chapter as a reference source.

When people are asked if they know any English spelling rules, they often claim that there are no rules, or quote, " 'i' before 'e', except after 'c'." The latter is only part of a rule and, unless you know the second half, it isn't a very reliable rule. (You can read more about this rule in Chapter 14.) Yet most adults probably do know some rules, although they may be unaware they have such knowledge.

Knowledge of rules

As children, learning to read and write, we probably began to make our own generalisations about the language and unconsciously became aware of some patterns.

EXAMPLES:

quack	queen	queasy
question	quibble	quick
quiver	quote	squirrel

What do you notice about these words?

'q' is always followed by 'u'; 'q' is always followed by another vowel after 'u'.

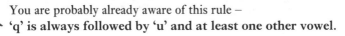

You are probably already aware of this rule –
'q' is always followed by 'u' and at least one other vowel.

Anyone who plays Scrabble is painfully aware of this fact because if you are unfortunate enough to pick up the only 'q' in the game, valued at 10 points, you will be unable to use it unless you also have a 'u' and another vowel among your tiles.

The sound made by the letters 'qu' used to be written 'cw' in words like 'cwen' for queen and 'cwic' for quick. When the Normans came to settle in Britain, they introduced Norman French and 'qu' was adopted, replacing the Anglo Saxon 'cw'.

The words below are nonsense words but if you came across them in a book you would be able to read them and you would pronounce them according to your previous knowledge of English sound patterns. Try reading them and then check your pronunciation with our suggestions.

hife	ludge	kneg	vack
sitchen	yake	hation	phento

Suggestions

hife would probably be pronounced with a long ī sound to rhyme with wife, strife, life.

ludge may rhyme with 'fudge' and 'trudge'. You probably didn't sound the 'd' and made the 'ge' sound like 'j'.

kneg was probably pronounced 'neg'. You opted to make 'k' silent.

vack could be pronounced in the same way as the words 'back', 'sack', and 'hack'.

sitchen immediately reminds us of 'kitchen'. You probably didn't pronounce the 't'.

yake may have been pronounced to rhyme with 'rake', 'sake' and 'lake'.

hation immediately reminds us of 'nation' as it is visually similar. You might choose a 'shun' ending because of your knowledge of similar 'tion' endings.

phento perhaps would begin with an 'f' sound, followed by 'en' and might end with an ō sound - 'fĕntō'.

In order to read these words, you have unconsciously applied 'rules' based on your knowledge of spelling patterns. You have recognised possible silent

6

letters, long and short vowel sounds and the probable sound that a given combination of letters may make.

Why are rules useful?

▶ One rule can apply to hundreds, even thousands of words.

▶ It is easier to remember a group of words that follow a pattern than to learn each word within the group.

▶ When you are proof-reading your writing and feel uncertain about a word, you can check it against the appropriate rule.

▶ Rules can give people confidence. They enable them to understand the structure of the language.

The problems caused by rules

▶ Rules are often long or complicated and so difficult to remember.

▶ There are frequently exceptions to rules.

▶ It can be difficult to remember the exceptions.

▶ For some rules it is impossible to give a definitive list of exceptions and you have to use the word 'generally' in the rule.

Helpful Hints

It's not enough to learn the rule by heart; you need to understand how it works and put it into practice.

▶ Try out each rule you learn. Test words to see if they fit the rule.

▶ Learn and practise one rule at a time.

▶ Be selective about the rules you learn. Prioritise them. Learn those which will help you with your problem words.

▶ Learn the rules which are simple to remember, which apply to a large number of words and have few exceptions.

▶ Rules or patterns are more meaningful if you can spot them yourself. Write down your own 'rules' as you discover them.

▶ When you read about a rule, try to express it in your own words. It is easier to recall then.

▶ When there is a list of exceptions to the rule, you need only learn those that are useful to you and that you will use frequently.

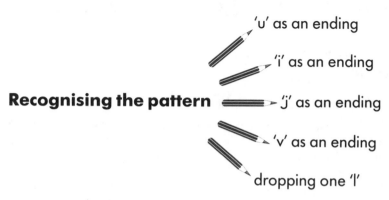

Recognising the pattern

'u' as an ending

'i' as an ending

'j' as an ending

'v' as an ending

dropping one 'l'

'u' is an unusual ending for words in English

EXAMPLES:

Peru	emu	guru
↓	↓	↓
from Spanish	from Portuguese	a Hindustani word

English words do not usually end in 'i'

An ī sound at the ends of words is usually made by 'y' or 'ie'.

6

EXAMPLES:

shy	die
supply	lie
apply	pie
occupy	tie

On the rare occasions that 'i' does appear at the end of an abbreviated or foreign word, it is not usually pronounced as an ī but as an ē.

EXAMPLES:

taxi is an abbreviation of taxicab

mini is an abbreviation of miniature

ski is a Norwegian word

macaroni, spaghetti, vermicelli and confetti are all Italian words

'j' is not an English ending

e.g. raj is a Hindustani word.

A 'j' sound at the end of words will be written 'dge' or 'ge'.

EXAMPLES:

edge	huge
acknowledge	fringe
smudge	revenge

'v' never ends words in English

'v' can appear at any place in a word but it is never the last letter. If you read the words below aloud they all have a 'v' sound at the end but each time it is followed by an 'e' which is silent.

EXAMPLES:

have	save	receive
cove	nerve	valve

'spiv' appears to be an exception to this rule but it is a slang word.

Dropping one 'l'

At the end of words

All these words have the same ending. What do you notice about each ending?

fretful	peaceful	useful	cheerful	beautiful
careful	wasteful	handful	spoonful	faithful

In these words, **full** has only one 'l'.

When 'full' is added to the end of a word, one 'l' is dropped.

Such a rule is very useful as it is simple to remember and applies to a large number of words. It also helps you to work out how many 'l's are needed when a word ends in 'ly'.

EXAMPLES:

merciful	+	ly	——►	mercifully
grateful	+	ly	——►	gratefully
boastful	+	ly	——►	boastfully

Helpful Hints

▶ handful   spoonful   basketful   cupful

If you want to make such words plural, then an 's' is added to the end of the completed word.

EXAMPLES:

two **handfuls** of rice

three **spoonfuls** of honey

four **basketfuls** of flowers

five **cupfuls** of flour

▶ skilful   wilful   fulfil

There is an extra point to remember for each of these words. Not only has 'full' dropped one of its 'l's but one 'l' has been dropped from 'skill', 'will' and 'full'.

skill	+	full ——▶	skilful
will	+	full ——▶	wilful
full	+	fill ——▶	fulfil

At the beginning of words

If you read these words you will hear **all** at the beginning of each.

almost   already*

although   also

altogether*   always*

When 'all' is added to the beginnings of words, one 'l' is dropped.

all	+	most ——▶	almost
all	+	ways ——▶	always

(To read more advice about the words marked with an asterisk, see Chapter 17.)

welfare   welcome

An 'l' disappears from 'well' at the beginnings of these words.

(But note 'farewell'. Both 'l's are needed here.)

Testing the rules

** Use your knowledge of rules outlined in this chapter to unscramble these anagrams.

rangqulead	a four-sided courtyard	gelloce	a place of study
kriqu	an odd habit	bbagace	green vegetable
kaque	to quiver with fear	danbgea	to wrap round a wound

ltiqu	a bed cover	voed	a bird
uueeq	to wait in a line	bvoea	over
qchuee	you may pay for goods with this	rvsee	to wait on someone
ylre	depend upon	ufoclourl	to be full of colour
preyl	answer	ntfluiple	abundant
yrt	attempt	gforfluet	absent-minded
edgnu	a gentle dig with the elbow	ghalmity	all powerful
gebad	you may wear one on your lapel	mstoal	nearly

As you check each word, recall the rule that applies to it.

** Sort these words into groups. Each group should follow one of the rules mentioned in this chapter.

questionnaire	hedge	spiteful
useful	thankfully	quarantine
twelve	pocketful	thoughtfully
curve	plunge	quell
pledge	reserve	masterful
painfully	deprive	judge
picturesque	try	change
fly	squabble	cry
wage	attractive	sinful

If you find it difficult to remember all these rules now, don't despair. Keep coming back to this section so that you can try out one rule at a time. By discovering the structure of the language you will provide yourself with a framework for your spelling and English will not seem such an illogical language.

If you give yourself sufficient practice and experience in the various sound patterns and rules, you will begin to see what is probable and possible in English spelling.

Remember, it doesn't matter how you recall the spelling of a word. Use different techniques according to the word you are learning. The important thing is that you eventually become a better speller.

7
Using Dictionaries

Why use a dictionary?

Nobody who writes should be without a dictionary, as everyone needs to use a dictionary at some time to check the spelling of a word. If you are concerned about your spelling then a dictionary is essential. It will not teach you how to spell but it will enable you to check the words you are worried about. Used sensibly, it can increase your confidence when you are writing as you know you have a reference source at hand.

Choosing a dictionary

There is an excellent choice of dictionaries on the market and it is advisable to spend some time looking at a range of dictionaries before making your choice. Listen to the advice of others by all means but then make your own decision as the choice of a dictionary is very personal. You need to find one that suits your needs and is easy for you to use.

You may decide that you need more than one dictionary: a larger, more detailed one for reference use at home, and a pocket dictionary or spelling dictionary to carry with you for on-the-spot checking. Although it is tempting to buy a cheap 'special purchase' dictionary, it is often false economy as there might be only a limited range of words, incomplete or misleading definitions, and no help with inflexions (word variants, e.g. cancel – cancelled, cancelling, cancellation). It is best to buy a dictionary produced by one of the leading publishers.

Types of dictionaries

▶ Spelling dictionaries
▶ Pocket dictionaries
▶ Concise dictionaries
▶ Phonetically arranged dictionaries

Spelling dictionaries

These are specialist dictionaries which include more entries than other dictionaries of similar size by simplifying definitions and omitting multiple meanings and word derivations.

This is a page from *The Pan Spelling Dictionary*.

cambium growing layer in a stem
cambric fine thin cloth
came pt. of **come**
camel animal with hump(s) used in the desert
camel-hair
camellia evergreen shrub
Camembert rich soft cheese
cameo stone with a raised design
cameos
camera apparatus for taking photographs
cameraman
Cameroonian of Cameroon
camion low four-wheeled truck
camisole old-fashioned underbodice
camomile or **chamomile** herbal plant
camouflage to conceal by disguising
camouflaging
camp (to set up) a temporary stopping- or sleeping-place
camper
campaign 1. set of military operations 2. plan of action
campaigner
campanile bell tower
campanology science of bell-founding and bell-ringing
campanologer campanologist
campanula plant with bell-shaped flowers
camphor strong-smelling substance
camphorated
campion common flowering plant
campus school or university grounds
campuses
can[1] to be able or allowed to
cannot can't could
can[2] (to put into) a metal container
canned cannery canneries canning
canal (to make) a channel, esp. through land
canalization canalize canalled canalling
canapé thin piece of bread or toast with savoury spread
canard false rumour
canary small yellow song-bird
canaries
canasta card game

cancan type of dance
cancel to cross out; to put off
cancellation cancelled (U.S. canceled) cancelling (U.S. canceling)
cancer diseased growth in the body
cancerous
Cancer Crab, constellation and zodiac sign
candelabrum branched candlestick
candelabra
candid [same sound as **candied**] frank
candidate person applying for a job, etc.; person taking an examination
candidacy candidature
candied [same sound as **candid**] preserved in sugar
candle wax rod with a wick for light
candlelight candlestick candlewick
candour (U.S. **candor**) frankness
candy (to) preserve in sugar; sweet
candies
candytuft garden plant
cane (to beat with) stem of certain plants
caning
canine to do with dogs; strong pointed tooth
canister small metal box
canker spreading infection or rot
cankerous cankerworm
canna tropical plant
cannabis drug from Indian hemp
cannibal one who eats human flesh
cannibalism cannibalistic cannibalize
cannon [same sound as **canon**] large heavy gun
cannonade cannonading cannonball cannonry
cannot = can not
canny shrewd
cannier canniest cannily canniness
canoe (to travel by) a light boat
canoed canoeing canoeist
canon [same sound as **cannon**] 1. church decree 2. principle 3. body of writings 4. list of saints 5. member of a cathedral chapter
canoness canonical canonically canonization canonize canonizing
cañon see **canyon**

Each word is laid out clearly and a very simple definition is given; just sufficient to ensure that you have chosen the correct word.

Other useful spelling dictionaries are *The Oxford Spelling Dictionary* (Oxford University Press), and *The Penguin Spelling Dictionary* (Penguin). Both books contain over 60,000 entries, with each entry divided into syllables, but no meanings are given.

Pocket dictionaries

A small pocket dictionary obviously contains fewer details under each entry but it is a convenient size and if you are using it to check the spelling of words then you do not need detailed information about their meanings.

A page of *The Pocket Oxford Dictionary* is shown in this chapter under the heading 'Guide words' and a single entry under 'Understanding an entry'.

Concise dictionaries

Examples of widely available concise dictionaries are *The Concise Oxford Dictionary* (OUP), *The New Penguin English Dictionary* (Penguin) and *Chambers Concise Dictionary* (Chambers).

These are more complicated to use than spelling dictionaries or pocket dictionaries as they have more entries to sort through and contain more information under each entry, but it is valuable to have one at home as a reference source.

It is unlikely you will need a more detailed dictionary than a concise version at home and if you want to look up a more unusual word or need more in-depth information, it is best to go to a library to consult larger volumes.

Phonetically arranged dictionaries

Overleaf is a page from *The Pergamon Dictionary of Perfect Spelling* (SRA Ltd). Some people find such dictionaries helpful as the entries are spelt to accord with their pronunciations.

For example, if you wanted to look up 'pneumonia', you may forget about the silent 'p' at the beginning and search under 'n'. You may also decide that the beginning should be spelt 'new'. If you looked this up, you would find 'newmonia' in coloured print and the correct spelling 'pneumonia' beside it in black print. Coloured print denotes the phonic spelling of the word, black the accepted spelling.

'pneumonia' can also be found under 'p' for the user who really knows how to spell the word but just wants to check.

Harraps also produce a phonetic dictionary, *Word Spell - A Spelling Dictionary*.

nesesitey	necessity⁺	next /-of-kin	
neslin	nestling	nexus	
nest¹ /ling		ni	nigh
net³ /ball		nibble²	
netha	neither	nibul	nibble²
nether		nice /ly/ness/r/st	
nettle² /rash		nicet y /ies	
netul	nettle²⁺	nich	niche
network		niche	
neumatick	pneumatic	nick¹	
neural/gia		nickel	
neuritis		nickerbockers	knickerbockers
neurologist		nickers	knickers
neuron		nickle	nickel
neuro *sis* /tic		nicknack	knick-knack
neuter		nickname²	
neuton	newton	nicotine	
neutral /ity		niece	
neutralis *e*² /ation		niether	neither
neutron /s		nifarious	nefarious⁺
neva	never⁺	nifarius	nefarious⁺
never /more/theless		nife	knife²⁺
nevu	nephew	niftie	nifty⁺
new* (not old) /er/est		nift y /iness	
new	gnu*	nigerd	niggard⁺
new	knew*	niggard /ly	
newclear	nuclear	niggl *e*²/y	
newcleus	nucleus⁺	nigh	
new *comer* /fangled		night *†/dress/gown	
new *ly* /ness		† (the dark)	
newmatic	pneumatic	night	knight†
newmonia	pneumonia	night *fall* /jar	
newral	neural⁺	nightingale	
newritis	neuritis	nightmare *e* /ish	
newrologist	neurologist	night-*shift* /-time	
newron	neuron	night-watch /man	
newrosis	neurosis⁺	nigle	niggle²⁺
newrotic	neurotic	niglect	neglect²⁺
news /agent/-flash		nigul	niggle²⁺
news *paper* /print/y		niks	nix
newt		nilon	nylon
newter	neuter	nimble /ness	
newton		nimblie	nimbly
newtralise	neutralise²⁺	nimbly	
newtron	neutron	nimbul	nimble⁺

Use your dictionary sensibly

Don't

▶ Depend on your dictionary too much. It will actually sap your confidence in your ability to spell. You will start to doubt yourself and check words that don't present problems.

▶ If you are uncertain about the spelling of a word, don't immediately search through your dictionary for it.

Do

▶ Try to write the word.

▶ If it looks wrong, write alternative versions. As you work through this book you will become aware of the alternative ways of making the same sound and gain the ability to base your 'guess' on other words with similar sounds or patterns.

▶ When you have completed your attempts, use a dictionary to check.

▶ Always complete your piece of writing before you use your dictionary. If you look up each word as you write, you will lose the flow and forget what you want to say. Writing will then become a chore.

▶ Train yourself to establish a set routine for writing.

Writing steps

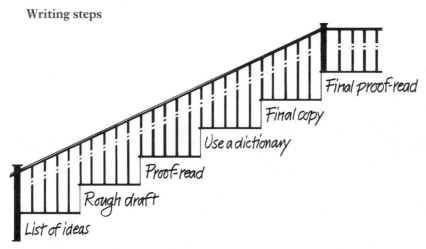

Final proof-read
Final copy
Use a dictionary
Proof-read
Rough draft
List of ideas

Step 1 **Make a note of all the points** you want to include in your writing.

Step 2 Write a rough copy. If you are uncertain of the spelling of a word, **write down your own attempt. Underline** it so that you can check it when you proof-read your work. If you cannot even attempt the spelling of

---

a word, **leave a space**. You can fill in the missing word later when you use your dictionary at the end. You will know which word you intend to write from the context of the sentence.

Step 3 Read your work through and check the **sense** of what you have written, the **punctuation** and the **spelling**. You can check these three points in any order but you may need to proof-read your rough draft more than once. It is a good idea to have a separate check for spelling.

Step 4 Use your dictionary to **check the words you have underlined** and to **work out the words that you have left spaces for**. You may find that you are able to attempt them more easily now that you have finished writing and can concentrate on them.

Step 5 Produce your final, **perfect version**.

Step 6 Give your writing **one last proof-read** to catch any errors you may have missed.

When you check a word in your dictionary, make certain it is the word you require by checking its definition.

This is particularly important with the many words which sound the same but are spelt differently according to their individual uses (homophones).

e.g. coarse   course

rough or vulgar   direction or route to be taken

Remember, you learn to spell in order to write. Write first, check your spelling later.

Dictionary skills

▶ Using an alphabetical sequence
▶ Working out the beginnings of words
▶ Working through words
▶ Saying the word
▶ Scanning skills
▶ Understanding an entry

People sometimes complain that dictionaries are too difficult to use and that they can never find the word they want, while others say dictionaries are too complicated. These are valid points but if you choose your dictionary carefully and practise using it, it will become a valuable tool.

When you buy or use a new dictionary, spend some time studying its contents, paying special attention to the first few pages which explain how the dictionary is arranged and the abbreviations and symbols used in it. You need not read all of these explanations thoroughly but you should be aware of their existence so that you can refer to them as you use your dictionary. There are often several pages of useful information at the end too.

Using an alphabetical sequence

Arrangement

All entries in a dictionary are arranged in alphabetical order with each letter having its own section. Within each of these 26 sections the words are also arranged in alphabetical order.

Although you will be familiar with the sequence of the letters in the alphabet, you may find certain sections present difficulties when you are using a dictionary. You may discover yourself reciting "h,i,j,k,l" in order to check whether 'k' comes before 'l' or 'j'. It is a good idea to spend some time improving your familiarity with the alphabet – this will enable you to use a dictionary more quickly as finding words can be very time-consuming.

When we are tired or worried we don't function as efficiently as usual so if you want to jog your memory, make a bookmark for your dictionary with the 26 letters written in order.

ABCDE FGHIJKLM NOPQRS TUVWXYZ
a bcde fghijklm nopqrs tuvwxyz

If you think of your dictionary as being divided into four quarters you will be able to find the letter you want more readily.

Rest your dictionary on its spine and divide the pages into two sections. The dictionary will fall open at the half-way mark, probably at the letter 'M'. If you then divide the first half into two sections, it will open at 'D' or 'E'. Divide the second half of the dictionary in a similar way. It will perhaps open at 'S'. If you try this several times with different dictionaries, the results will be very similar.

A - E will form the first quarter

F - M will form the second quarter

N - S will form the third quarter

T - Z will form the final quarter

Deciding which quarter you need can reduce the time you spend searching for a word. You can divide your bookmark into quarters too if you think it will help.

Guide words

At the top of each page or double page there are two guide words.

etc.; subdued expression of discontent; softly spoken or nearly inarticulate speech. 2. *v.i.* & *t.* Make murmur; utter (words) softly; complain in low tones. 3. ∼ous *a.*, with murmuring sound. [F or L]

mūr′phy *n.* (sl.) Potato. [Ir. surname]

mŭ′rrain (-rǐn) *n.* Infectious disease in cattle; (arch.) a ∼ (plague) **on you!** [AF *moryn*]

mŭ′sca|dīne *n.* Musk-flavoured kind of grape; ∼t *n.*, (wine made from) muscadine; ∼tĕl *n.*, muscat, raisin from muscadine. [MUSK]

mŭ′scle (-sel). 1. *n.* Any of the contractile fibrous bands or bundles that produce movement īn animal body (**not move a** ∼, be perfectly motionless); that part of the animal body which is composed of muscles, chief constituent of flesh; (muscular) power; ∼-**bound**, with muscles stiff and inelastic through excessive exercise or training; ∼-**man** (with highly-developed muscles, esp. as intimidator). 2. *v.i.* (sl.) ∼ (in), intrude by violent means. [F f. L dim. of *mus* mouse]

Mŭ′scov|īte *n.* & *a.* (arch.) Russian; (citizen) of Moscow; ∼ȳ *n.*, (arch.) Russia; ∼y duck, MUSK-*duck*. [L (*Moscow*)]

mŭ′scŭlar *a.* Of or affecting muscle(s); having well-developed muscles; *muscular* DYSTROPHY; **mŭs-cūlǎ′rǐtȳ** *n.* [MUSCLE]

mūse¹ (-z) *v.i.* & *t.* (literary). Ponder, meditate, (*on, upon*); say meditatively. [F]

mūse² (-z) *n.* The M∼s, (Gk & Rom. Myth.) nine sister goddesses, inspirers of poetry, music, drama, etc.; **the** ∼, poet's inspiring genius; **mūsē′um** (-z-) *n.*, building used for storing and exhibition of objects illustrating antiquities, natural history, arts, etc., (∼um piece, specimen of art, manufacture, etc., fit for a museum, old-fashioned person or machine etc.). [F or L f. Gk *mousa*]

proverbial for rapid growth (∼ **growth** etc., sudden development, thing suddenly developed); (fig.) upstart; ∼ (**cloud**), cloud of mushroom shape, esp. from nuclear explosion. 2. *v.i.* Gather mushrooms; spring up rapidly; expand and flatten like a mushroom cap. [F *mousseron* f. L]

mū′sǐc (-z-) *n.* Art of combining sounds of voice(s) or instrument(s) to achieve beauty of form and expression of emotion; sounds so produced; pleasant sound, e.g. song of bird, murmur of brook, etc. (∼ **to one's ears**, something very pleasant to hear); (written or printed score of) musical composition(s); ‖ ∼-**hall**, (place for) singing, dancing, variety entertainment, etc.; *music of the* SPHEREs; ∼-**paper** (with printed staves for writing music-score); ∼-**stool** (with adjustable height of seat, for pianist); **face the** ∼, face one's critics etc., not shirk consequences; **rough** ∼, noisy uproar, esp. with vexatious intention; SET¹ (poem etc.) *to music*; ∼**al**, (*a.*; -lly) of music, (of sound etc.) melodious or harmonious, fond of or skilled in music, set to or accompanied by music, (‖ ∼**al box**, instrument that plays certain tunes mechanically; ∼**al chairs**, a boisterous party game in which players are eliminated through failing to find seats when music stops; ∼**al comedy**, light dramatic entertainment with songs; ∼**al film**, in which music is important feature; *musical* INSTRUMENT; ∼**al saw**, bent saw played with violin bow; ∼**al sound**, produced by continuous regular vibrations), (*n.*) musical film or comedy; ∼**ian** (-I′shan) *n.*, person skilled in science or practice of music; ∼**ŏ′logȳ** *n.*, study of music other than that directed to proficiency in performance or composition; ∼**olŏ′gǐcal** *a.*; ∼**ŏ′logǐst** *n.* [F f. L f. Gk (MUSE²)]

mŭsk *n.* Substance secreted by male musk-deer used as basis of perfumes; plant (formerly) with musky smell;

This shows you that 'murphy' is the first word on the page and 'musk' the last word. All words between 'murphy' and 'musk' will appear on this page. When you work through the dictionary looking for a word, use the guide words to help you. They will speed up your search.

** Try this out for yourself with the following words. Don't forget to use the guide words and quarters to help you.

rapier	exercise	carbon	sewage
anxious	maximum	terylene	entrance

Working out the beginnings of words

"How can I look up a word if I don't know how it begins!" is a familiar cry. You need to know the first few letters in order to be successful.

Vowels

Words which begin with a vowel can cause problems because the initial sound of the word is not stressed.

'a' and 'u', 'e' and 'i', 'a' and 'o' are easily confused so if your word sounds as if it begins with a vowel and you cannot find it under one vowel, look under another.

's', 'c' or 'k'?

It is not only the vowels that present problems.

▶ e.g. ceiling

Here a search could well take place under 's'. Knowing about soft and hard 'c's (Chapter 13) would stop you making this mistake.

▶ e.g. chaos

This word can be difficult to find. The first letter sounds like 'k'. Knowing which combinations of letters can make a particular sound will help you to look up the word under the various alternatives.

▶ e.g. the 'k' sound at the beginning of words can be written

c (canoe, cartridge)

k (kangaroo, kidnap)

ch (chemist, choir)

Silent letters

e.g. knobbly

A search under 'n' would be unsuccessful as 'k' is silent. Knowing about possible silent letters (Chapter 5) can prevent you making this mistake.

As you work through the chapters, you will begin to appreciate the combinations of letters that can make a particular sound.

Working through the word

Middles

The middle of words can also cause problems but generally they are easier to deal with than word beginnings.

e.g. ordinary

Here the 'din' may be confusing. A search could be conducted under 'ordenary'. Again, you know it is a vowel sound so look under alternative vowels. It isn't too difficult once you are in the section where words begin with 'or'.

Endings

e.g. ordinary

Sometimes last letters of a word cause difficulty. You will need to look under the various vowel alternatives. Once you get to the ends of words it is easier to check the alternatives as you already have so much of the word to help you. Having reached the 'ordin...' point in the dictionary there are only a few words to check through.

Saying the word

When you are looking up a word, use your knowledge of dividing words into syllables (Chapter 4). This will allow you to concentrate on one part of the word at a time. Say the word aloud and then write down the syllables.

e.g. con/cen/trate

You can then try to work through each syllable, letter by letter.

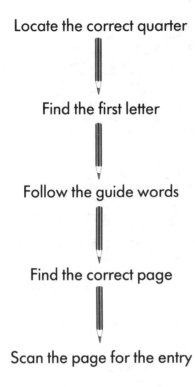

Locate the correct quarter

Find the first letter

Follow the guide words

Find the correct page

Scan the page for the entry

Once you have located the correct page, you need to scan quickly down the list of words to find the exact word you want. You need a quick, alert eye so that you can find the word quickly. We put great emphasis on finding a word quickly because if you can find words readily you are far more likely to use your dictionary for checking.

Understanding an entry

Overleaf is an entry from *Chambers Concise Dictionary*. You will notice that under the entry **deck** there are other words associated with the main word, e.g. **decked** and **decker**. If you wanted to find the spelling of **decked** there would not be a separate entry for the word. You have to be prepared to look under the root word. As each root word within the word group is in bold type, it is easy to scan through the entry.

deck *dek*, *v.t.* to clothe: to adorn: to furnish with a deck.—*n.* a horizontal platform extending from one side of a vessel to the other, thereby joining them together, and forming both a floor and a covering (*naut.*): a floor, platform, or tier as in a bus, bridge, etc.: the ground (*slang*): a pile of things laid flat: a pack of cards: the part of a pack used in a particular game, or the undealt part: the turntable of a record-player: that part of a tape-recorder or computer in which the magnetic tapes are placed, and the mechanism for running them: a set of punched cards.—*adj.* **decked** (*dekt*) adorned, decorated.—*ns.* **deck'er** the person or thing that decks: a vessel, vehicle, or other structure that has a deck or decks (used only in composition, as *three-decker*); **deck'ing** adornment: a platform.—**deck'chair** a chair, usually folding and made of canvas, such as passengers sit or lie on deck in; **deck'-hand** a person employed on deck: an ordinary sailor; **deck'-house** a house, room, or box on deck; **deck'-passage** a passage securing only the right of being on deck, without cabin accommodation; **deck'-pass'enger**; **deck'-quoits** quoits as played on a ship's deck, with rope rings; **deck'-tenn'is** lawn-tennis modified for playing on board ship.—**clear the decks** to tidy up, remove encumbrances, esp. in preparation for action (orig. naval action, now often *fig.*); **hit the deck** (*slang*) to lie, fall, or be pushed down quickly. [Verbal meanings—Du. *dekken*, to cover; substantive meanings—M. Du. *dec*, roof, covering.]

Note also that the pronunciation is given after each entry.

e.g. deck *dek*, decked *dekt*

The part of speech is also indicated.

e.g. deck v.t. (verb)

Slang expressions associated with the root word are given.

e.g. hit the deck

The origins of the word are given at the end of the entry: Dutch and Middle Dutch.

** Dictionary practice

Use your dictionary to find the missing letters in these words. Consider alternative vowels, silent letters and alternative combinations of letters for a particular sound.

dung...on	rei...burse	fl...orescent
pit...ful	capsi...e	correspond...nce
effi......ent	suspi......ous	para......el
duplicat...r	misc...llan...ous	extr...vagant
surv...illance	dimen...ion	depend...ble

Compare these two entries for the word 'travel'.

travel *trav'l*, *v.i.* to journey: to go: to go round soliciting orders: to move along a course: to go with impetus: to be capable of withstanding a journey: to move.—*v.t.* to journey over or through:—*pr.p.* **trav'elling**; *pa.t.* and *pa.p.* **trav'elled**.—*n.* journeying.—*adj.* **trav'elled** having made journeys: experienced: frequented.—*n.* **trav'eller** one who travels or has travelled: one of the travelling people: one who travels for a mercantile house: a piece of mechanism that moves on a gantry, etc.—*n.* and *adj.* **trav'elling**.—*n.* **travelogue** (*trav'ə-log*) a talk, lecture, article, or film on travel.—**travel agency** an agency which provides information, brochures, tickets, etc., relating to travel; **travel agent**; **traveller's cheque** a cheque which can be cashed at any foreign branch or specified agent of the bank issuing it; **trav'eller's-joy** *Clematis vitalba*, sometimes called old man's beard; **travelling folk, people** the name by which itinerant people often call themselves, in preference to the derogatory names gipsies or tinkers.—*adj.* **trav'el-sick** suffering from travel sickness.— **travel sickness** nausea experienced, as a result of motion, by a passenger in a car, ship, aircraft, etc. [**travail**.]

tră'vel. 1. *v.t.* & *t.* (‖-ll-). Make journey(s) esp. of some length to distant countries, traverse (country, distance) thus, (*ordered to travel for his health*; *has travelled the world*); (colloq.) withstand long journey (*wines that travel badly*); act as COMMERCIAL traveller (*for* firm, *in* commodity); (of machine or part) move *along* bar etc., *in* groove etc.); pass esp. in deliberate or systematic manner from point to point (*his eye travelled over the scene*); move, proceed, in specified manner or at specified rate (*travels at 600 m.p.h.*; *light travels faster than sound*); (colloq.) move quickly; ~ling bag, small bag carried by hand, for traveller's requisites; ~ling clock, small clock in a case; ~ling crane (moving on esp. overhead support); * ~ing salesman, commercial traveller.

This entry is from *Chambers Concise Dictionary*. A large, detailed dictionary obviously gives you more information and is particularly useful when you want to check the spelling of a word like 'travel' which changes (by adding a second 'l') in the words 'travelled', 'travelling', and 'traveller'. Each word is given.

This entry from *The Pocket Oxford Dictionary* shows a bold 'll' after the entry, indicating that two 'll's are needed in some words but the words are not listed.

** Homophones

Find the differences in meaning between these pairs of words.

wave	waive
council	counsel
bail	bale
review	revue
shear	sheer

** Plurals

Find the plurals of these words.

buffalo	synopsis
index	oasis
salmon	memorandum
cactus	criterion
phenomemon	gateau

Creating your own dictionary

If you are serious about improving your spelling, it is essential to keep your own personal dictionary or word list. You can use a small note book or loose-leafed folder and divide it into alphabetical sections. It is better to divide a note book yourself than buy one that is already alphabetically arranged, so that you can allow more space for some letters than others. You may prefer to use a small box with index cards and enter one word on each card.

Whichever system you choose, you can enter words under the relevant letter. Obviously you will not be able to achieve alphabetical order within each letter as you will list the words as they occur. You can choose to enter all the words you encounter that you cannot spell, or selected problem words. It may be useful to have two books, one for reference with less common words and a small pocket book for everyday use.

Remember it isn't enough to devise an efficient filing system for your words, you must also learn the spelling of the words. Sort out your priority words and learn a few of these at a time.

Using a spell check

If you use a word processor you may have one with a spell-check facility. This can be a useful aid for spotting typing or spelling errors. Your word processor may bleep if you type in a word incorrectly, or you may have a device for checking a single word or your complete document at the end. Use this facility if you have it but be aware of its shortcomings.

The word processor will only be able to deal with the words that have been programmed into its dictionary so some perfectly acceptable words may be questioned.

It will not be able to differentiate 'practice' from 'practise' or 'their' from 'there'. If you have spelt the word correctly, it will not mind that you have chosen the wrong word for the context. So proof-read your typing and use a dictionary in conjunction with your spell check.

Final thoughts

Don't let looking up a word be too much bother. Excuses like "The print is too small"; "I can never find the word I want"; "It is impossible to use a dictionary when you don't know how the word begins"; "It takes too long" can all be overcome. If you choose the right dictionary, follow the guidelines, and practise, you will find a dictionary is an invaluable reference tool.

8
Jogging the Memory

We all have individual ways of remembering information. Some of us would have difficulty remembering the number of days in a given month without the rhyme

> 30 days hath September
> April, June and November.
> All the rest have 31
> Excepting February alone
> Which has 28 days clear,
> And 29 each leap year.

Compass directions are easy to remember if you know

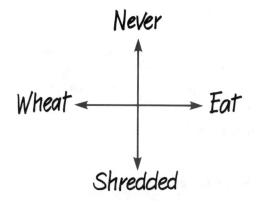

The order of the colours of the rainbow can be recalled by: **Richard of York gave battle in vain** (red, orange, yellow, green, blue, indigo, violet).

Such rhymes and phrases jog our memories and provide a useful aid when we need to recall information. It is often helpful to invent similar aids to remember difficult spelling patterns.

Mnemonics

A mnemonic is a verse or other device to help the memory.

You will probably find that the most useful mnemonics are those you devise yourself but sometimes recalling someone else's mnemonic for a problem word can help.

EXAMPLES:

necessary – **one** collar and **two** socks

embarrassment – **two** red cheeks and **two** scarlet ears.

the CID investigates accidents and incidents.

add an **add**ress to your letter.

all the vowels in cemetery are 'e's.

Mnemonics are helpful for

▶ Silent letters

▶ Difficult double letter combinations

▶ Rules and exceptions to rules

▶ Homophones

Silent letters

When learning to spell words containing silent letters, it is helpful to group the words together.

If you can then devise a memorable sentence for these words, it may help you to recall the problem letter or letters more easily.

For example, if you wanted to remind yourself of some silent 'k' words, then the sentence

The knight knew the knack of knitting knickers.

might help you!

Visualising the knight and his knitting may make the mnemonic more meaningful and reinforce the spelling pattern. The more bizarre the picture you create, the more memorable the spelling pattern becomes.

** Perhaps you can think of sentences for these groups of silent letter words.

1 ghost	whisky	exhibit	whisper
2 autumn	condemn	column	government
3 guard	guest	guitar	guarantee
4 castle	listen	fasten	whistle
5 plumber	numb	thumb	dumb
6 write	wrong	wretch	wriggled

Difficult double letter combinations

You may find it helpful to remember difficult letter combinations in a word by identifying the problem letters and chanting them to yourself as you write the word.

EXAMPLES:

Two 'c's and two 'm's in acco**mm**odation.

Two 'm's, two 't's and two 'e's in committee.

Two 'c's but one 's' in occasion.

One 'c' but two 'm's in reco**mm**end.

Spelling rules

Mnemonics can also help you recall words connected with spelling rules more easily.

In Chapter 14 the 'i' before 'e' rule is explained. An amusing rhyme for remembering some of the 'ei' spellings is

> The wicked bandit
> Who practised deceit
> Gazed at the ceiling
> And seized the receipt.

Similarly, a list of exceptions to the rule for final 'e's and consonant suffixes can perhaps be more easily remembered by

> Truly, Mr Duly, your ninth argument is wholly awful and that's the truth

In all the coloured words you would expect an 'e' to be present if the words followed the rule. See Chapter 12 for this rule and others like it.

Homophones

Memory aids can also help you work out which of a pair of homophones to use.

Homophones are words which sound alike but have different spellings and different meanings. (See Chapter 15.)

e.g.   stationary   stationery

        remaining still   paper, envelopes, etc.

Think of this sentence if you have difficulty remembering which word refers to writing materials and which word means not moving:

A stationery shop sells envelopes.

e.g.　　　　　principal　　　　　　　　　　principle

　　　　head of a college　　　　　a fundamental truth
　　　　or university

A useful mnemonic for distinguishing between these two words is:

A college principal can be a good pal.

**The homophones below can cause confusion. Try to devise sentences to identify the words within each pair.

source/saucer	sight/site	draft/draught
currant/current	drawers/draws	dual/duel
hole/whole	weather/whether	which/witch

Which mnemonic to use?

You have already been shown several different ways to remember spelling patterns. Some may be more useful to you than others. They may suit your way of learning or they may be more appropriate to the type of words you wish to learn. However, by looking further at the various types of mnemonic and how each can be used, you will be able to select the right memory aid for both you and the word.

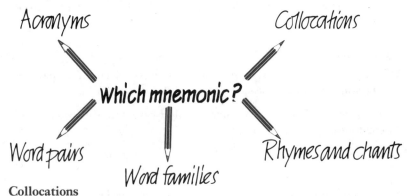

Collocations

These are groups of words often seen together which can be used to emphasise a spelling pattern.

EXAMPLES:

high and **migh**ty ('igh' spelling)

a **great deal** ('ea' spelling)

a **rui**ned **sui**t ('ui' spelling)

here, **there** and everyw**here**. (The word 'here' appears within each of these 'place' words.)

We **hear** with our **ear**s. ('hear' and 'here' can cause confusion so use this sentence to remember which to use.)

** By using this technique, it may be possible to find a 'partner' for each of these words.

horr<u>ible</u>	d<u>ou</u>ble	fur<u>ious</u>
w<u>eigh</u>t	dist<u>urb</u>	dam<u>age</u>

Rhymes and chants

As the rhyme about the wicked bandit shows, a rhyme or chant can help you to recall a particular spelling pattern.

e.g. Carg**oes** of potat**oes** and tomat**oes**.

This phrase is useful to remind you of the 'oes' endings of each of these words.

A chant can be equally memorable. Try reading these words aloud and rhythmically saying each letter name.

ic-ic-les

M-i-ss-i-ss-i-pp-i

Obviously, the most successful chants are based on repetitive patterns of letters. However, some people find that chanting (even silently) the letters of any tricky word can help with the spelling.

Try these:

mur–mur	murmur
bag–gag–e	baggage
mi–ni–mum	minimum
q–ue–ue	queue
ba–na–na	banana
on–i–on	onion

8

Word families

When learning spelling patterns, developing word families can be a good quick memory aid.

e.g. travel

 travel**ler**

 travel**ling**

 travel**led**

Here, the 'er', 'ing' and 'ed' endings are added after doubling the 'l'. Instead of learning each word separately, by recognising the pattern and remembering it, you get 'three for the price of one'.

** Identify the pattern in each of these word families and try to find more examples for each family.

technical	picturesque	vague
technician	technique	fatigue
technology	cheque	league

whimper	usual	comic
rhubarb	manual	frantic
exhausted	actual	dramatic

Word pairs

It can be useful to learn certain words in pairs. Such pairings are often only meaningful or useful to the person who devises them, but it is worth being aware of this technique. It can be used for words which have the same spelling pattern or to emphasise a pair of words sounding alike but having different spelling patterns.

e.g. different and difficult

Both of these words start with 'diff'.

e.g. similar and familiar

It is easy to confuse which of the two words ends in 'iar'. By remembering the pair and exaggerating the 'i' sound before the 'ar' sound in 'familiar', it becomes easier to identify which is which.

e.g. separate and desperate

Again, the words in the pair obey different spelling patterns and confusion may arise as to which is spelt 'ar' and which 'er'. Try to remember them as a pair and stress 'separate' but 'desperate' when trying to recall which spelling pattern to choose.

** You may like to try this technique with these word pairs which can cause problems.

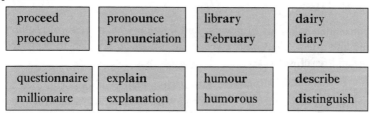

| proceed procedure | pronounce pronunciation | library February | dairy diary |

| questionnaire millionaire | explain explanation | humour humorous | describe distinguish |

Acronyms

These words are made up from the initial letters of other words.

EXAMPLES:

radar comes from the words 'radio detection and ranging'.

scuba (as in scuba diving) comes from 'self-contained underwater breathing apparatus'.

posh from 'port outward, starboard home'. This acronym is supposed to have originated from the desire of wealthy visitors to India to have cabins on the ship's port side during the outward journey but occupy starboard cabins for the return journey to Britain.

If you have difficulty spelling a word, try treating it as an acronym and then find a word for each letter of your problem word.

e.g. guilt

You could remember this by:

green   underwear   is   less   tempting

g   u   i   l   t

e.g. sigh

Sid   is   Greta's   hero

s   i   g   h

This technique works for fairly short words but it is obviously difficult to apply to longer words.

** See if you can find acronyms for these words.

shoe	juicy	worst	our
enemy	sugar	only	any

Word games

These provide a stimulus to practise and develop your mastery of spelling patterns and rules. They also give you a variety of practice to reinforce patterns and recall words you have been learning.

There are several word games available and plenty of opportunities in newspapers and magazines for completing word puzzles, many of which can provide a valuable focus for words and heighten your awareness of vocabulary and spelling.

Scrabble and lexicon

These games provide an opportunity for you to form words by using your knowledge of possible letter combinations. However, the letters on the tiles or cards are shown in capitals. It may be helpful to try out the spelling on paper first, as capital letters don't give a good visual image.

Crosswords

These reinforce your knowledge of letter order and enable you to recognise probable letter patterns. For example, if the first two letters you have for a word are 'zl', it is likely you have made a mistake!

Anagrams

An anagram is a word with the letters in the wrong order. Unscrambling it may help you to analyse the letter order and remember the correct spelling of a word.

** Try to sort out these words. The first letter of each answer is underlined.

ehwn	malc	soed	urdgin
oneutg	ihghte	nocoup	pploee
delobu	oucnis	xiansou	chbrouer
eeaaurntg	chae	cpnltuua	chblroea
spptieoo	pssriuer	uelva	fiieetnd

Words within words

In Chapter 4 you were encouraged to look for a word within a longer word to help you remember the spelling pattern. This word game, in which you try to find as many words as possible from one long word, won't necessarily help you to spell that longer word but may make you look more carefully at words and their letter patterns. It may also encourage you to use your dictionary to check the spelling of any of the words you have found that you aren't sure of.

e.g. surprising

This word contains these words and probably many more: sing, in, ring, uprising, rising, pursing, spring, grip, spin, spun, pun, grin and purr.

** See how many words you can make from each of the following words.

appetite   document   conversation   labelled

Creating your own word games

Perhaps you could create your own word games. Here are some ideas.

Word chain

Write down a fairly short, simple word and then develop a word chain from it by changing a letter, leaving out a letter or adding a letter each time.

e.g. ace
 face
 fate
 late
 slate
 slat
 slot
 blot
 bloat
 float
 floats

** Try creating a chain from each of the following words.

band   like   know   swing

Word square

Here you start with a blank grid and you have to choose your own words to fill it. The last two letters of each chosen word must become the first two letters of the next. The square is completed in a clockwise direction.

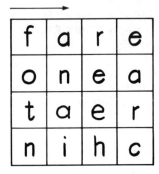

In this square, the first word was 'fare', the second 'rear', third was 'arch', fourth 'chin', fifth 'into', sixth 'tone', the seventh 'near' and the eighth 'area'.

You might choose a word ending in two letters which form an impossible combination to start the next word, e.g. wing, jump or sews. Use your knowledge of possible word beginnings when choosing words.

Final thoughts

All of us have some words which we find tricky. It is hoped that the techniques outlined in this section will help you to find ways of remembering the spelling of your own problem words. Choose the method which you find most helpful and suitable for you and then apply it to your words. It works!

As you work through Section 3, you will find further advice about using techniques. If the techniques we recommend for certain words work for you then use them; if not, use one or more of the other methods. Remember, it doesn't matter how you learn the words, the only important thing is that your spelling improves.

9

Short and Long Vowels

In Chapter 4 you were given some information about vowel sounds and asked to identify short and long vowel sounds in given words. This chapter looks at short and long vowels in more detail and shows some of the ways such sounds can be made. Understanding short and long vowels will help you with the rules for suffixing in Chapter 12 and the pronunciation of words.

The symbols used in this chapter are the *breve* (˘) which denotes a short vowel sound and the *macron* (¯) to show a long vowel sound.

What is a short vowel sound?

You have already learnt that each vowel has a short sound which is different from its letter name. Listen to the short sound made by the vowels shown in colour.

ă	access	balance
ĕ	empty	pencil
ĭ	inch	omit
ŏ	object	proper
ŭ	until	sunny

When are vowels short?

In each of the words in the group above, the vowel printed in colour has a short sound because the syllable containing it ends in one or more consonants. The syllable is said to be 'closed'.

word	number of syllables	pronunciation	reason
access	2 syllables	ăc/cess	'c' closes the first syllable.
empty	2 syllables	ĕmp/ty	The first syllable is closed by 'mp'.
inch	1 syllable	ĭnch	'nch' closes the syllable.
proper	2 syllables	prŏp/er	'p' closes the first syllable.
bundle	2 syllables	bŭn/dle	The first syllable is closed by 'n'.

** Complete this table.

word	syllables	syllable containing underlined vowel	consonant/s closing that syllable
balance	bal/ance	bal	l
tax			
pencil			
tell			
omit			
winner			
object			
gossip			
until			
sunny			

As you have already seen, a vowel is short if the syllable ends in one or more consonants. Sometimes in one-syllable words it is difficult to know whether the word ends in one, two or even three consonants.

Guidelines for closed syllables
▶ Double consonants
▶ 'ck' or 'k'?
▶ 'dge' or 'ge'?
▶ 'tch' or 'ch'?

Double consonants

f	l	s	z

These consonants are usually doubled at the end of short vowel one-syllable words.

EXAMPLES:

cuff	well	mess	buzz
staff	pull	loss	fuzz

There are a few exceptions to this rule which are worth noting.

if	of	is	this
his	bus	us	has

ck or k?

In words of one syllable, use ck at the end if it is a short vowel sound and there is no other consonant sound before the final 'k' sound.

eg. **speck** has one syllable, an ĕ sound, and there is no other consonant sound before the final 'k'.

OTHER EXAMPLES:

back	wreck	quick	clock	struck
stack	check	brick	stock	pluck

The 'ck' spelling also occurs in words of two syllables where the 'k' sound closes the first short vowel syllable.

EXAMPLES:

rack/et	chick/en	sock/et	buck/et
jack/et	tick/et	sprock/et	jock/ey

OTHER EXAMPLES:

backing	wrecked	clocking	stacking
checked	bricking	stocked	plucking

Use k at the end of a word if there is another consonant sound before the final 'k' sound,

EXAMPLES:

bank has an 'n' before the 'k' sound.

talk has an 'l' before the 'k' sound.

or if there is a long vowel sound in the word.

EXAMPLES:

streak has an ē sound.

cloak has an ō sound.

** Fill in the spaces with either 'ck' or 'k'.

The interviewer spo___e to a number of people who were stri___en with grief when they heard of the disaster. Various people put their hands in their po___ets and insisted on ma___ing a donation to the fund. Several charities said they would put together a pa___age of aid which would include: tru___s, blan___ets and food pa___ets. The sho___ing news affected the sto___ mar___et, where dealers started to sell re___lessly and share prices suffered a setba___.

'dge' or 'ge'?

The 'j' sound at the end of words is spelt either dge or ge. If the word is of one syllable, contains a single short vowel sound and has no other consonant sound before the 'j' sound, this 'j' sound is spelt dge.

e.g. **badge** has one syllable, an ă sound, and there is no other consonant sound before the 'j' sound.

EXAMPLES:

edge	midge	dodge	nudge
ledge	ridge	lodge	budge

Note also these two–syllable words.

bu**dge**t	ga**dge**t	fi**dge**t

Remember, if there is another consonant sound before the 'j' sound, the word ends ge.

EXAMPLES:

flange	mer**ge**	cringe	forge	bul**ge**

'tch' or 'ch'?

Look at these one-syllable words.

ch	tch
search	match
punch	fetch
winch	stitch
drench	Scotch
march	Dutch
poach	hatch
peach	hitch
coach	botch
speech	clutch

When is the 't' required?

Follow the patterns for **ck/k** and **dge/ge** words. In one-syllable words containing a short vowel with no other consonant sound before the final 'ch' sound, use tch.

Use **ch** if there is either another consonant sound before the final 'ch' sound, or a long vowel sound in the word.

Two vowels combining to make a short vowel sound

So far in this chapter, you have been shown short vowel sounds being made by a single vowel. This is the norm, but there are certain occasions when two vowels combine to make a single short vowel sound.

'ea' makes an ĕ sound

In a number of words 'e' and 'a' combine to make an ĕ sound although, as you will see later in this chapter, 'ea' can also make an ē sound.

As many of the words where 'ea' makes an ĕ sound are commonly used, it is useful to recognise the pattern.

EXAMPLES:

head	sounds like	hĕd
bread	sounds like	brĕd
leather	sounds like	lĕther
health	sounds like	hĕlth
thread	sounds like	thrĕd
dealt	sounds like	dĕlt
sweat	sounds like	swĕt

** Unscramble these anagrams. All the words contain the 'ea' spelling making an ĕ sound. The first letter of the unscrambled word has been underlined.

lea<u>w</u>hty	rd<u>s</u>pea	yt<u>s</u>ead
rease<u>p</u>lu	fen<u>d</u>ea	eavy<u>h</u>
lous<u>j</u>ea	rent<u>t</u>hea	rdy<u>a</u>eal
the<u>f</u>ear	<u>d</u>frludea	po<u>w</u>ean

There are other examples of two vowels combining to make a short vowel sound. However, as they occur less frequently, these combinations appear only in the checklist at the end of this chapter.

Section 3

9

Vowel confusion

In a few words the short vowel sound is made by an unlikely vowel.

ŭ sound

among   oven   money

The ŭ sound made by an 'o' occurs in a number of words and can cause confusion for the speller.

EXAMPLES:

love	front	tongue	wonder
mother	company	month	none
come	done	won	does
some	comfort	nothing	other

The confusion between 'o' and 'u' stretches back through history. Nearly a thousand years ago the Normans, who invaded Britain from France, changed the spelling of some English words. One of the changes was to spell the ŭ sound with an 'o'. You will also find that the pronunciation of both short and long 'u' sounds in words varies according to the regional accent of the speaker.

Other less common instances of vowel confusion are shown in the checklist at the end of this chapter.

Although this chapter shows several exceptions, remember that the most common way of spelling a short vowel sound is by using the obvious single vowel.

What is a long vowel?

In each of the words below, the vowel printed in colour has a long sound: the same sound as its letter name.

ā	able	vacant
ē	evil	decay
ī	idle	final
ō	obey	photograph
ū	usual	popular

When are vowels long?

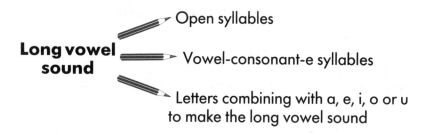

Long vowel sound
- Open syllables
- Vowel-consonant-e syllables
- Letters combining with a, e, i, o or u to make the long vowel sound

Open syllables

You have already been shown that vowels in closed syllables have a short sound. In the group of words listed on the previous page, the sound of the coloured vowel is long because the syllable actually ends in that vowel.

Syllables ending in a single vowel are open syllables and the vowel is usually long.

word	number of syllables	pronunciation	reason
able	2 syllables	ā/ble	The first syllable is 'a'.
decay	2 syllables	dē/cay	The first syllable ends in 'e'.
idle	2 syllables	ī/dle	The first syllable is 'i'.
photograph	2 syllables	phō/tō/graph	The first and second syllables end in 'o'.
popular	3 syllables	pop/ū/lar	The second syllable is 'u'.

Vowel–consonant–e syllables (silent 'e' words)

e.g.

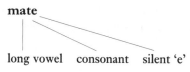

mate

long vowel   consonant   silent 'e'

In these syllables the final 'e' is silent but makes the single vowel that precedes it long. There can only be one consonant between the vowel and the 'e'.

This is a common pattern in words and one that you will need to recognise before suffixing rules are introduced.

Compare these pairs of words.

mǎt and māte	The ǎ in the first word in each
hǎt and hāte	pair becomes an ā when the silent 'e' is
spǎt and spāte	added.

sǐt and sīte	
fǐn and fīne	ǐ becomes ī after the silent 'e' is added.
spǐn and spīne	

mǒp and mōpe	
slǒp and slōpe	ǒ becomes ō after the silent 'e' is added.
cǒd and cōde	

cǔb and cūbe	
plǔm and plūme	ǔ becomes ū when the silent 'e' is added.
dǔd and dūde	

'e-consonant-e' is an unlikely combination in words of one syllable.
One example is 'here' but it is difficult to hear the ē sound as it combines
with 'r'. The long vowel sound is difficult to hear in other words where
there is an 'r' between the vowel and the silent 'e'.

EXAMPLES:

care	spire	bore	cure

** Try adding 'e' to the ends of these words and listen to the change of sound
in each case.

can	pin	rip	tub	not	cut	hat	hid
dot	bar	fat	hop	sham	rod	pip	spit

This silent 'e' pattern occurs in words of more than one syllable and in
different positions in words. However, it is more likely to be found at the
ends of words.

EXAMPLES:

frus/trate	a–e ending
brace/let	a–e at the end of the first syllable
pat/ron/ise	i–e ending
su/preme	e–e ending
ex/e/cute	u–e ending

** Complete these words with the correct vowel.

obsol_te	desper_te	sinc_re
am_se	comp_re	cons_me
sen_le	contrib_te	sev_re
conc_se	desp_te	esc_pe
concr_te	prom_te	sch_me
surv_ve	conf_se	introd_ce

Letters combining with a, e, i, o or u to make the long vowel sound

a

a-e is the most frequently used construction which makes an ā sound, but 'ai' and 'ay' can also be used.

'ai' makes an ā sound in the middle of words; the ā sound at the end of words is made by 'ay'.

EXAMPLES:

ai	ay
drain	day
strain	sway
afraid	affray
exclaim	clay
straight	stray

e

'ee' and 'ea' are the most common ways of spelling the ē sound in the middle of words.

Unfortunately there is no 'rule' to show which of these two combinations is correct in any given word. Any problem words will probably have to be learnt visually.

EXAMPLES:

ee	ea
greet	reach
indeed	cheap
breeze	conceal
between	reason
freeze	beneath
speech	speak

** Fill in the missing letters with 'ee' or 'ea'.

app_ _l	decr_ _sing	exc_ _d
disagr_ _able	f_ _ture	guarant_ _
proc_ _d	rep_ _ted	rev_ _ling
succ_ _ded	tr_ _ty	br_ _the

A few words with an ē sound at the end are spelt **ee**:

EXAMPLES:

licensee	coffee	committee	degree

but **y** usually makes the ē sound at the end of words.

In words like 'happy', 'very', 'monkey' and 'smoky' the final long ē sound is made by **ey** or **y**.

FURTHER EXAMPLES:

lonely	courtesy	casualty	agility
modesty	trophy	hasty	stony
donkey	jockey	chimney	turkey

Most words ending in an ē sound actually end with a 'y'.

Take care with words like 'safety' and 'lively'; the 'e' before the suffixes 'ty' and 'ly' can cause confusion. There is more on these suffixes in Chapter 12.

i

An ī sound at the end of words is usually made by a 'y'.

EXAMPLES:

fry	dry	my	why
July	apply	defy	identify
occupy	supply	terrify	rely

But ī is formed by **igh** in a few frequently used words. It makes a long ī sound at the end of these words:

high   sigh

and an ī sound within these words.

might	night	fight	tight
right	light	sight	bright
fright	plight	blight	flight

o

The most common spelling of the ō sound is the 'o–consonant–e' pattern shown earlier in this chapter. However, there are some frequently used words where the letters 'oa' or 'ow' make the ō sound

oa occurs in the middle of words.

EXAMPLES:

throat	foam	road	loaf	soap
coast	groan	goal	loan	float

ow occurs mainly at the end of words.

EXAMPLES:

slow	know	below	elbow
narrow	borrow	follow	swallow

However, occasionally this combination is found in the middle or beginning of words.

EXAMPLES:

own	owe	thrown	bowl

'ow' can have another sound, the 'ouch' sound. This is dealt with in Chapter 10.

u

The ū sound doesn't occur in many English words. As you have seen, it can be made by 'u–consonant–e' (e.g. confuse). A similar but not identical sound can be made by using **ue, ew, ui, ou** or **oo**. These letter combinations will be dealt with in Chapter 10.

Understanding short and long vowels is fundamental to knowing how words can be built up by their sound patterns. This chapter has shown you the most common ways in which such sounds are made. You will probably need to refer to this chapter as you work through the book in order to refresh your memory of these vowel sounds.

Section 3

9

Summary

Short vowel sounds occur in closed syllables and in the other instances shown below.

vowel sound	closed syllable	other instances
ă	băt/tle	
ĕ	lĕg/end	'ea' as in wĕalthy
ĭ	mĭn/ute	
ŏ	pŏs/i/tive	
ŭ	ŭm/pire	ŏ as in done

Long vowel sounds occur in open syllables and in the other instances shown below.

vowel sound	open syllable	other instances
ā	tā/ble	'a–e' as in ventilāte 'ai' as in explāin 'ay' as in betrāy
ē	bē/side	'e–e' as in complēte 'ee' as in agrēed 'ea' as in benēath 'y' as in nasty 'ey' as in hockey
ī	bī/cycle	'i–e' as in prīde 'igh' as in frīght 'y' as in supply
ō	hō/tel	'o–e' as in whōle 'oa' as in rōast 'ow' as in knōw
ū	stim/ū/late	'u–e' as in abūse (And see chapter 10)

Checklist

These are less common ways of making **short vowel sounds.**

vowel sound	letters	examples
ă	ai	plait
ĕ	ie	friend
	ai	said
	a	any, many
ĭ	ui	biscuit, build
	e	pretty
	o	women
	u	busy, business
	i–e	imaginative, give
ŏ	ou	cough, trough
	a	swan, squash
ŭ	oo	blood, flood
	ou	touch, rough

These are less common ways of making **long vowel sounds.**

vowel sound	letters	examples
ā	ey	obey, prey
	ei	neighbour, weigh
	au	gauge
	ea	break, steak
ē	ie	piece, believe
	ei	receipt, conceit
	i–e	routine, machine
ī	ai	aisle
	oi	choir
ō	oe	toe, hoe
	ough	although, though
	ou	boulder, shoulder
ū	See Chapter 10	

10
Same Sound, Different Spelling

Chapter 9 looked at different ways of making short and long vowel sounds. In this chapter you will once again be shown alternative ways of making sounds and given advice about

the various letter combinations,

the most likely combination to use, and

where the combinations occur within words.

What is the problem?

Listen to the 'or' sound in these words,

store

August

flaw

and to the 'er' sound in these words.

verse

girl

church

In each list one sound is made by more than one combination of letters. The difficulty is choosing the correct combination for the word.

Why is there a problem?

As Chapter 1 explained, in English we have 26 letters in the alphabet but they have to make approximately 44 different sounds. This means that letters have to be combined with each other to make sounds. Unfortunately, pronunciation and spelling have changed over the years. Pronunciation no longer matches spelling and we can have either a sound being made by several different letter combinations (as above) or a letter combination having a number of different sounds.

EXAMPLES:

coupon

though

cloud

Are there any rules?

It is possible to look at letter combinations and find some patterns in their use.

In Chapter 9 you were shown the 'ai' and 'ay' combinations.

<u>ai</u>	<u>ay</u>
aim	tray
plain	play
brain	delay
exclaim	dismay

Do you remember the rule?

'ai' is used at the beginning or in the middle of words; 'ay' at the end of words.

There are exceptions, but very few (e.g. mayor) so, if in doubt, apply the rule.

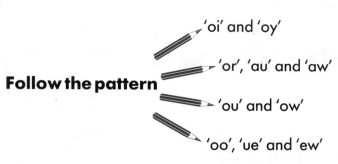

Follow the pattern

'oi' and 'oy'

'or', 'au' and 'aw'

'ou' and 'ow'

'oo', 'ue' and 'ew'

'oi' and 'oy'

Both of these combinations make the sound of 'oy' as in 'boy'.

**Based on your knowledge of the 'ai' and 'ay' rule, complete these words with 'oi' or 'oy'.

av_ _d	ann_ _	all_ _
_ _l	p_ _se	h_ _st
empl_ _	expl_ _t	_ _ntment
destr_ _	ch_ _ce	app_ _nt
cl_ _	embr_ _der	inv_ _ce
m_ _st	j_ _nt	enj_ _

You can check your answers but if you followed the pattern all the words will be correctly completed. Three important exceptions to remember are voyage, loyal and royal.

Perhaps you can devise a mnemonic for these exceptions.

'or', 'au' and 'aw'

The combination of the letters 'o' and 'r' ('or') is the most likely spelling of the 'or' sound in words.

EXAMPLES:

orphan

decorate

Norway

accord

perform

But 'au' and 'aw' can also make the 'or' sound.

Think of the 'ai' and 'ay' and the 'oi' and 'oy' patterns as you look at these words.

auburn	paw	jaw
automatic	naughty	outlaw
saw	daughter	saucer

Can you see a similar pattern?

'au' occurs at the beginning and middle of words; 'aw' at the end of words.

There are a few 'aw' exceptions, some of which are shown below. If you have difficulty with them, find a technique to help you learn them.

| dawn | bawl | awful |
| yawn | trawl | awkward |

** 'au' words tend to be longer and sometimes more difficult to spell than 'aw' words. Check your spelling of these 'au' words by filling in the missing letters.

f _ _ d	a swindle
g_ _z_	light material
_ud_b _ _	can be heard
au_ _ _ _ce	spectators
_ _d_tor	works with accounts
c_ _t_on	warning
_ _ _ti_ _	sale
a_th_ _ _ty	position of power
ap_ _ _ _se	a sign of enjoyment
aud_ _ _ _us	bold
h_ _l_e	heavy road transport

'ou' and 'ow'

As you have already seen in this chapter, 'ou' can have several different sounds. Both 'ou' and 'ow' can make an 'ouch' sound. (The polite word you might utter if you sat on a pin.)

EXAMPLES:

blouse	endow
found	brow
proud	allow
council	cow
ounce	sow
spouse	prow
sour	how

| Helpful Hints |

▶ 'ou' is never used at the end of a word; use 'ow'.

▶ 'ou' is more common in the middle of words.

▶ Sometimes 'ow' is found in the middle of words.

EXAMPLES:

scowl

crowd

vowel

Check in your dictionary if the word looks wrong even if you have used the guidelines.

'oo', 'ue' and 'ew'

These letter combinations make similar sounds, almost a ū sound.

EXAMPLES:

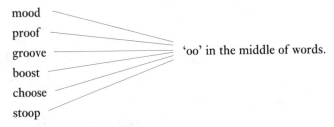

mood

proof

groove   'oo' in the middle of words.

boost

choose

stoop

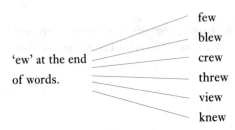

'ew' at the end   few

of words.   blew

crew

threw

view

knew

clue

queue

value   'ue' at end of words.

issue

subdue

continue

Helpful Hints

▶ If the last sound in a word is like a ū, use 'ew' or 'ue'.

▶ If the sound in the middle is like a ū, try 'oo'.

98

Sound problems

▶ One combination, several sounds
▶ Several combinations, one sound

One combination, several sounds

oo

EXAMPLES:

food

look

good

If you read these words aloud, you will hear the 'oo' combination making a slightly different sound in each word. This sound will also vary according to your accent. Take care with 'oo' words as the sound they make can be confusing; such words are often best learnt by visual techniques or mnemonics.

ough

This is the combination we all dread. The same combination of letters is pronounced very differently in individual words. Here are the most common 'ough' words arranged in groups according to the sound the 'ough' combination makes.

drought	tough	though
bough	enough	although
plough	rough	dough

| trough | borough | through |
| cough | thorough | |

| ought |
| thought |
| bought |
| fought |
| brought |

10

If you have difficulty with these,

    learn them in their groups,

    remember the words visually,

    or devise mnemonics for them.

augh

list 1	list 2
laugh	daughter
laughter	caught
	naughty
	taught
	slaughter

This is also a difficult combination. You can hear that the 'augh' sound in the words in list 1 is very different from the 'augh' sound in the words in list 2. There are no rules which can be generally applied; you will have to find other ways of remembering them.

Several combinations, one sound

Sounds like ū

In the first part of this chapter you were shown 'oo', 'ue', and 'ew' words, all having a sound similar to ū in them. There are three other combinations that also make a similar sound. Although they do not occur as frequently, they are useful to recognise.

ou	ui	eu
soup	bruise	feud
coupon	suitable	sleuth
youth	juice	
route	fruit	

You can see that these combinations occur in the middle of words, so you can generally rely on the ū sound at the end of words being spelt either 'ue' or 'ew'. Unfortunately there is no rule to help you to decide which of these

---

three combinations to use in the middle of words.

If in doubt, write the word down, spelling it in several ways,

decide which looks right,

apply the rules you know and think about what is probable

then check your spelling in a dictionary.

'ur', 'ir', 'er' and 'ear'

Each of these four combinations can make an 'er' sound within words.

EXAMPLES:

blur   shirt   kerb   earn

> **Helpful Hints**

▶ 'er' is the most common combination for the 'er' sound at the end of words.

▶ 'ur' is more common than 'ir'.

▶ 'ear' is used least.

** Test yourself with these words. Use 'ur', 'ir', 'er' or 'ear' to complete each word.

th........st	sw........ve	conc........n	p........pose
s........prise	p........chase	n........ve	dist........b
s........vice	s........ch	s........geon	sub........b
m........ge	s........name	........nest	s........vive
........gent	memb........	........ly	bett........
c........cle	f........niture	suff........	sk........t

'f', 'ff', 'gh' and 'ph'

These are the four ways of making an 'f' sound.

	at the beginning of the word	in the middle of the word	at the end of the word
f	form	often	beef
	few	lift	leaf
	fear	after	chief
			Hint: Use 'f' after a long vowel.
ff		suffer	stuff
		offer	gruff
		traffic	bluff
		coffee	stiff
		Hint: Learn such words by syllabification.	Hint: Use 'ff' after a short vowel.

Can you see any patterns in these words where both 'ph' and 'gh' make a 'f' sound?

pheasant	phrase	pamphlet	biography
physics	microphone	nephew	autograph
symphony	tough	rough	triumph
laugh	enough	emphatic	phobia

Guidelines

▶ 'ph' makes an 'f' sound in many more words than 'gh'.

▶ 'ph' can be at the beginning, in the middle or at the end of words.

▶ 'gh' making an 'f' sound occurs in the middle or at the end of words.

▶ 'gh' is a problem sound in English – you have already seen bough, ought, tough, etc.

▶ The 'h' can also be silent in words like ghastly, ghetto and ghost.

Although, as the 'gh' spelling illustrates, English spelling appears to lack rules, you should by now be aware of many instances when spelling does follow quite clear guidelines. The knowledge of possible alternatives and spelling patterns helps you to make informed choices and can make you feel more confident about your spelling as you write.

A checklist of sounds

sound	possible letter combinations				
or	or	au	aw		
	more	autumn	claw		
er	er	ir	ur	ear	
	weather	girl	burst	earth	
oy	oi	oy			
	coil	employ			
'ouch'	ou	ow			
	sound	now			
oo/ū	oo	ue	ui	ou	eu
	booth	value	cruise	through	feud
f	f	ff	ph	gh	
	feet	cuff	physics	laugh	

11
How to Form Plurals

singular	plural
denotes one person or thing	**denotes more than one**
target	targets
responsibility	responsibilities
bush	bushes
business	businesses
thief	thieves
chief	chiefs
radio	radios
hero	heroes
daughter-in-law	daughters-in-law
ox	oxen
stratum	strata
aircraft	aircraft

Are there patterns for making words plural?

In Chapter 6 you were advised to concentrate on rules which were easily learnt, covered a large number of words and had few exceptions. Some of the most useful rules to learn are those concerning making words plural. Once you know the guidelines you can tackle unfamiliar words with confidence and success.

The simplest and most common way to form the plurals of nouns is to add 's' to the singular.

garden	picture	handbag	nest	option
gardens	pictures	handbags	nests	options

'Hiss' at the end

EXAMPLES:

porch

fox

kiss

waltz

bus

lash

If you say these words aloud, you will notice that although they do not all end in the same letters or make exactly the same final sound, there is a 'hiss' at the end of each word. In the plural these words become

porches

foxes

kisses

waltzes

buses

lashes

It would be very difficult to pronounce such words if just an 's' were added to each of them, and impossible to hear a difference in sound between the singular and plural forms.

If a noun ends in ch, sh, s, ss, x, z or zz, an 'es' must be added to make the word plural.

EXAMPLES:

singular	plural
guess	guesses
bunch	bunches
atlas	atlases
address	addresses

You will notice that by adding 'es' you are adding another syllable to each word.

guess	(one syllable)	guess/es	(two syllables)
bunch	(one syllable)	bunch/es	(two syllables)
at/las	(two syllables)	at/las/es	(three syllables)
ad/dress	(two syllables)	ad/dress/es	(three syllables)

11

** Sort out the words from the columns below which have hissing or sibilant endings and then make each word plural.

expectation	chorus	bench	arch
gas	cross	hoax	fez
witness	six	thought	peach
ash	larynx	boss	crash
box	stress	chest	coach
stitch	pest	flower	buzz
Christmas	latch	mattress	tax

'y' at the end

Nouns ending in 'y' frequently cause problems but there is no need as the rule is simple and there are no exceptions to it.

Can you work out the rule? (It involves the letter before the 'y'.)

chart 1		chart 2	
authority	authorities	kidney	kidneys
party	parties	convoy	convoys
enquiry	enquiries	display	displays
ally	allies	essay	essays
galaxy	galaxies	trolley	trolleys
spy	spies	holiday	holidays
bully	bullies	journey	journeys
cherry	cherries	key	keys
library	libraries	toy	toys
enemy	enemies	buoy	buoys

chart 1	chart 2
▸ Each word has a consonant before the final 'y'.	Each word has a vowel before final 'y'.
▸ All the words in the plural end in 'ies'.	All the words in the plural end in 's'.

If there is a consonant immediately before the 'y', change 'y' to 'i' and add 'es'.

If there is a vowel before the 'y', just add 's' to the word.

** century   delay   valley   activity

   opportunity   turkey   reply   chimney

   monkey   factory   alloy   donkey

   dictionary   fly   relay   anxiety

Think about the letter before the final 'y' in each of these words before you make the word plural and place it in the correct column.

ies	s
e.g. babies	abbeys

'ff', 'f', or 'fe' at the end

singular	calf	safe	chief	half	life	gulf	cliff
plural	calves	safes	chiefs	halves	lives	gulfs	cliffs

Words that end in 'ff' are simple to deal with in the plural.

EXAMPLES:

cuffs   muffs   puffs   tariffs

Words ending in 'f' or 'fe' are more difficult. As you can see from the list above, **some words form their plurals by adding 's';**

EXAMPLES:

safes   chiefs   gulfs

in others 'f' becomes 'v' and 'es' is added.

EXAMPLES:

calves   halves

Plurals ending in 'ves'

chart 3	
self	selves
elf	elves
shelf	shelves
wolf	wolves
thief	thieves
loaf	loaves
leaf	leaves

11

chart 3 (continued)	
sheaf	sheaves
calf	calves
knife	knives
wife	wives
life	lives
half	halves

All other words add 's' to form the plural

EXAMPLES:

roof	roofs
proof	proofs
belief	beliefs
reef	reefs

Ways of remembering the pattern

▶ You could learn that all nouns ending in 'f' or 'fe' add 's' except the thirteen in chart 3.

▶ You could link some of the words in chart 3 to make rhymes to help you remember the list.

EXAMPLES:

The <u>thieves</u> stole the <u>loaves</u> from the <u>shelves</u>.

His <u>wives</u> have had <u>knives</u> all their <u>lives</u>.

The <u>sheaves</u> were in <u>halves</u> so the <u>calves</u> hid them<u>selves</u> under the <u>leaves</u> to escape the <u>wolves</u> and the <u>elves</u>.

▶ These are ideas but it is usually more effective if you make up your own rhymes.

▶ If you emphasise the pronunciation of the end of the word, this will help you to remember its spelling pattern.

Either way will do

A few words can have either form in the plural.

dwarfs	or	dwarves
scarfs	or	scarves
turfs	or	turves
hoofs	or	hooves
wharfs	or	wharves

'o' at the end

buffaloes	radios
volcanoes	trios
heroes	discos
mosquitoes	kangaroos
tomatoes	solos

Some words which end in 'o' add 's'; others add 'es' in the plural.

You could generalise and say that all nouns ending in 'o' add 's' and then learn a very long list of exceptions, but learning such a list is difficult and you may never need to use some of the words in the list. It is probably better to concentrate on other methods.

Ways of remembering the pattern

▶ If there is a vowel before the final 'o', add 's'.

EXAMPLES:

kangaroos   radios   shampoos   cuckoos   studios   zoos

▶ Make up your own rhymes to remember groups of words ending in 'es', (for example, in Chapter 8 we showed you the mnemonic '*cargoes* of *potatoes* and *tomatoes*').

▶ Nouns which have been abbreviated add 's'.

EXAMPLES:

discos   photos

▶ Nouns taken from Italian or Spanish add 's'.

EXAMPLES:

sombreros   ponchos   solos

▶ Nouns associated with music add 's'.

EXAMPLES:

pianos   cellos   sopranos   concertos

Either way will do

For some words either ending is acceptable.

EXAMPLES:

Eskimoes	Eskimos
stilettoes	stilettos
mottoes	mottos

'es' words

These are some of the more common words ending in 'es'; perhaps you can form them into groups and devise a mnemonic to help you remember them.

embargoes	mangoes	potatoes	tomatoes
dominoes	volcanoes	mosquitoes	buffaloes
heroes	tornadoes	echoes	cargoes

e.g. The *heroes* played *dominoes* among the *mangoes*.

Irregular plurals
EXAMPLES:

man	men	tooth	teeth
woman	women	foot	feet
child	children	mouse	mice
goose	geese	louse	lice

Such words are frequently used and well known so they do not usually present problems for the native English speaker.

No change
Some words are the same in both the singular and the plural form.

EXAMPLES:

deer	pants
sheep	trousers
salmon	scissors
trout	mathematics
grouse	series
moose	species
news	tights
cattle	innings
fish *or* fishes	

Compounds

EXAMPLES:

singular	plural
man-of-war	men-of-war
passer-by	passers-by
son-in-law	sons-in-law
court-martial	courts-martial
maid-of-honour	maids-of-honour

Here the main word in the group is made plural. In the following words both parts are judged to be of equal importance.

manservant	menservants
woman writer	women writers

Foreign words

Some words taken from other languages still keep their original plural forms.

EXAMPLES:

singular	plural
stimulus	stimuli
radius	radii
medium	media
criterion	criteria
phonomenon	phenomena
larva	larvae
crisis	crises

Other words can have two plural forms: the original spelling and an anglicised one.

EXAMPLES:

singular	original plural	anglised plural
terminus	termini	terminuses
memorandum	memoranda	memorandums
syllabus	syllabi	syllabuses
fungus	fungi	funguses
formula	formulae	formulas

11

bureau	bureaux	bureaus	
gateau	gateaux	gateaus	
plateau	plateaux	plateaus	

Apostrophes

The main uses of apostrophes are:

▶ to show that letters are missing, e.g. don't (the 'o' from 'do not' is missing).

▶ to indicate the owner.

EXAMPLES:

My son's bike has been stolen.

The employees' jobs had been axed.

Apostrophes are not used to make nouns plural.

Combining the guidelines

** Use the guidelines outlined in this chapter to complete the columns below.

singular	plural	singular	plural
bye-law		circus	
	tweezers	oasis	
blush		guy	
axis			hippopotami
	lice	brooch	
	canaries	mouse trap	
tattoo			lenses
potato		ditch	
	leaves	colliery	
wife		beach	
thief			corridors
	stories	gangway	
scientist		storey	
	tidings	discovery	
byway			tongs
pocketful			criteria
igloo		currency	
	rodeos	class	

12
Adding Endings

In Chapter 11 you were shown how to make singular nouns plural, by adding 's' or 'es'. You will have seen that sometimes the spelling of a word changes when it is made plural. This chapter looks at other types of word endings (suffixes) and how, when they are added to words, they can affect spelling.

What is a suffix?

suffix, a syllable or other addition at the end of a word:

(from Chambers Twentieth Century Dictionary)

A suffix added to a word doesn't necessarily change the meaning of the word but makes the base word fit the way we wish to use it in the sentence.

e.g. Come here <u>immediately</u>! (Base word 'immediate' plus the suffix 'ly'.)

Examples of suffixes

There are many different letter combinations which can be added to the ends of words, some of which are shown below.

suffix	example of use	base word
let	booklet	book
hood	neighbourhood	neighbour
ing	waking	wake
ed	shopped	shop
ment	advertisement	advertise
ly	quickly	quick
ful	beautiful	beauty
ee	employee	employ
ise/ize	visualise/ize	visual
y	tasty	taste

Section 3

12

The same suffix can be added to a variety of words.

EXAMPLES:

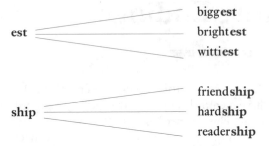

est ———— biggest
———— brightest
———— wittiest

ship ———— friendship
———— hardship
———— readership

Sometimes two suffixes are added to a word.

EXAMPLES:

joyfulness   (ful and ness)

effortlessly   (less and ly)

Many long words become easier to spell if they are split into syllables. By recognising suffixes and knowing how they are added to words, you will find the syllabification technique even more useful.

Are there any rules?

If you look back to the examples already given you will see that:

▶ In some instances the suffix is added directly to the base word with no change made to the spelling.

EXAMPLES:

quick + ly ——▶ **quickly**.

employ + ee ——▶ **employee**.

▶ In other examples the spelling of the base word changes.

EXAMPLES:

beauty + **ful** ——▶ **beautiful** ('y' changes to 'i').

taste + **y** ——▶ **tasty** (the 'e' is dropped).

▶ In another case the final consonant of the base word is doubled.

e.g. shop + **ed** ——▶ **shopped** (the 'p' is doubled).

There are clear rules which account for these changes. These rules are very useful to know and understand as they cover a large number of words and

---

114

have few exceptions. Spelling mistakes can occur when suffixes are added to words because the speller is unaware of or uncertain of the rules. By knowing these rules, you will feel more in control of your spelling.

Although you may at first glance think that the rules are wordy and difficult to remember, once you practise them you will find them more useful. It doesn't matter if you don't remember a rule word for word so long as you can put the idea into practice.

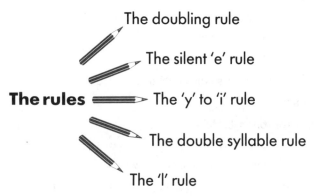

The rules
- The doubling rule
- The silent 'e' rule
- The 'y' to 'i' rule
- The double syllable rule
- The 'l' rule

The doubling rule

This rule deals with base words where there is

▶ **one** syllable
▶ **one** short vowel
▶ **one** final consonant

e.g. **wet** has one syllable,

one short vowel, 'e', and

one final consonant, 't'.

If a suffix beginning with a vowel is added to a 'one, one, one' base word, the final consonant of the base word is doubled.

EXAMPLES:

wet + **er** ⟶ wetter (the suffix starts with a vowel, 'e').

wet + **ing** ⟶ wetting (the suffix starts with a vowel, 'i').

Remember a 'y' is also a vowel suffix.

e.g. **chat** + y ⟶ chatty

When a suffix beginning with a consonant is added, don't double the final consonant of the base word.

EXAMPLES:

wet + **ness** ──▶ wetness (the suffix starts with a consonant, 'n').

wet + **ly** ──▶ wetly (the suffix starts with a consonant, 'l').

For the doubling rule to apply the word must fit the pattern exactly.

Checking the pattern

EXAMPLES:

Does feed have one syllable?✓

one short vowel?✗ ('ee' makes an ē sound)

one final consonant?✓

There are only two ticks so the doubling rule doesn't apply.

(feed + **ing** ──▶ feeding)

Does sell have one syllable?✓

one short vowel?✓

one final consonant?✗ (two 'l's)

There are only two ticks so the doubling rule doesn't apply.

(sell + **er** ──▶ seller; sell + **ing** ──▶ selling.)

Does show have one syllable?✓

one short vowel?✗ (ō)

one final consonant?✓

There are only two ticks so the doubling rule doesn't apply.

(show + **ed** ──▶ showed; show + **y** ──▶ showy.)

It may seem a little tedious at first to keep checking for the 'one, one, one' pattern but it soon becomes automatic.

** Add the suffix to the base word in each of the examples below.

base word	suffix	base word	suffix
stop	ed	bank	ing
clean	est	jam	ed
explain	ing	slim	est
flat	ly	glad	en
wrap	er	dust	y
shut	ing	grin	ed
fun	y	scar	ed

base word	suffix	base word	suffix
thin	er	crisp	y
swift	er	see	ing
fret	ing	plan	er

** Remove the suffix from these words and write the base word.

dragging	sunny	failing
bigger	scrapped	gunner
madness	dimly	swimmer
sipping	bidders	blotted
risky	stepping	dropped
flipped	harder	faster

As you have already seen, a 'q' is always followed by 'u'. As these two letters are always seen together, they count as one letter when you check 'qu' words against the 'one, one, one' rule.

EXAMPLES:

quit + **ing** ⟶ quitting (the 'i' is short, so double the 't').

quip + **ed** ⟶ quipped (the 'i' is short, so double the 'p').

quick + **er** ⟶ quicker (the word ends in two consonants, so don't double).

queer + **est** ⟶ queerest (the 'e' is long, so don't double the 'r').

The silent 'e' rule

This rule concerns those words which end in a silent 'e'. Can you work out the rule?

list 1			list 2		
rate	ed	rated	hate	ful	hateful
place	ing	placing	tire	some	tiresome
spice	y	spicy	blame	less	blameless
stride	ing	striding	fate	ful	fateful
invite	ation	invitation	excite	ment	excitement

The silent 'e' is dropped when a vowel suffix is added but kept when a consonant suffix is added. Remember 'y' can be a vowel too.

** Add the suffixes to each word below. Remember to consider whether the suffix begins with a vowel or a consonant.

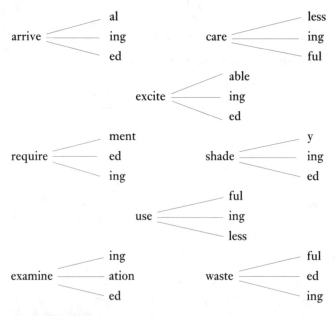

arrive — al / ing / ed

care — less / ing / ful

excite — able / ing / ed

require — ment / ed / ing

shade — y / ing / ed

use — ful / ing / less

examine — ing / ation / ed

waste — ful / ed / ing

> ### Helpful Hints

There are a few exceptions to the silent 'e' rule and if they are learnt, whole groups of words become easier to spell.

Base words ending in 'ce' or 'ge'

In order to keep 'c' and 'g' soft (sounding like 's' and 'j') in words like 'notice', 'manage' and 'courage' when 'able' or 'ous' is added, the 'e' is retained.

noticeable

manageable

courageous

If the 'e' were dropped, 'c' and 'g' would occur before an 'a' or an 'o' and would have a hard sound. (See Chapter 13 for more on hard and soft 'c's and 'g's.)

Words retaining the 'e' before a vowel suffix

There are a few other words where 'e' is kept before a vowel suffix.

EXAMPLES:

acreage	dyeing
singeing	gluey

Other words can be spelt with or without the 'e'.

EXAMPLES:

rateable	or	ratable
sizeable	or	sizable
likeable	or	likable
saleable	or	salable
loveable	or	lovable
ageing	or	aging
queueing	or	queuing
mileage	or	milage

In American spelling the 'e' is usually dropped in such words and this is gradually becoming more acceptable in English spelling. If you are unsure, try checking the word in a dictionary – but you may find that in this instance different dictionaries have different ideas!

Words which drop 'e' before a consonant suffix

In these words the final 'e' of the base word is dropped before the consonant suffix is added.

base word	word plus consonant suffix
argue	argument
awe	awful
nine	ninth
true	truly and truth
whole	wholly
due	duly

The mnemonic quoted in Chapter 8 may help you to remember these words.

'Truly, Mr Duly, your ninth argument is wholly awful and that's the truth.'

You have been shown several exceptions to the silent 'e' rule, but on most occasions the silent 'e' is dropped before a vowel suffix and kept before a consonant suffix.

12

The 'y' to 'i' rule

In Chapter 11 you were shown how to make words ending in 'y' plural.

EXAMPLES:

authorities	kidneys
parties	convoys
enquiries	displays
allies	essays

When you make words which end in 'y' plural, those which have a consonant before the 'y' change the 'y' to 'i'. If the word has a vowel before the 'y', there is no change.

Look at these two lists. Is the pattern followed when other suffixes are added?

list 1	list 2
'heavy' and 'ness' becomes 'heaviness'	'display' and 'ed' becomes 'displayed'
'pretty' and 'est' becomes 'prettiest'	'betray' and 'al' becomes 'betrayal'
'apply' and 'ed' becomes 'applied'	'survey' and 'ing' becomes 'surveying'
'mystery' and 'ous' becomes 'mysterious'	'repay' and 'ment' becomes 'repayment'
'pity' and 'ful' becomes 'pitiful'	'destroy' and 'ing' becomes 'destroying'
'busy' and 'ly' becomes 'busily'	'obey' and 'ed' becomes 'obeyed'

The pattern is followed regardless of whether the suffix begins with a vowel or a consonant.

If the base word has a consonant before the final 'y', change the 'y' to 'i' when adding a suffix. If there is a vowel before the final 'y', add the suffix without changing the 'y'.

But don't change 'y' to 'i' when adding 'ing'.

EXAMPLES:

carry has an 'r' before 'y'.

Add **er** and it becomes **carrier**;

add **ed** and it becomes **carried**;

but add **ing** and it becomes **carrying**.

empty has a 't' before 'y'.

Add **ed** and it becomes **emptied**;

add **er** and it becomes **emptier**;

but add **ing** and it becomes **emptying**.

There are very few exceptions to this rule:

lay becomes laid

pay becomes paid

day becomes daily

gay becomes gaily

** Complete the columns below using the guidelines.

base word	add ing	add er
destroy	destroying	destroyer
tidy		
worry		
copy		
convey		
buy		
steady		

base word	add ly	add est
noisy	noisily	noisiest
lazy		
easy		
ready		
crazy		
happy		

Section 3

12

base word	add ed	add es
multiply	multiplied	multiplies
apply		
deny		
hurry		
terrify		
accompany		
weary		

The double-syllable rule

Look at the words listed below. They each have

▶ Two syllables

▶ One final consonant

▶ One short vowel before the final consonant

or/der	en/ter	lim/it
bud/get	pi/lot	mar/ket
prof/it	al/ter	dif/fer

You may hear, as you read each word, the stress falling on the first syllable. If you have difficulty with this, say the word aloud or use the word in a sentence and listen to which part of the word sounds stronger. You should hear

order	enter	limit
budget	pilot	market
profit	alter	differ

When adding a vowel suffix or a consonant suffix to words where the first syllable is stressed, do not double the final consonant of the base word.

EXAMPLES:

order and ing becomes ordering

budget and ed becomes budgeted

limit and less becomes limitless

The words listed on the next page also have

    Two syllables

    One consonant at the end

    One short vowel before the final consonant

oc/cur	e/quip	pre/fer
for/get	for/bid	re/gret
com/mit	trans/mit	o/mit

When you read each of these nine words, you should hear the stress falling on the second syllable; the voice becomes louder and stronger towards the end of the word.

occur	equip	prefer
forget	forbid	regret
commit	transmit	omit

When adding a vowel suffix to words where the stress falls on the second syllable, double the final consonant. Don't double the consonant when adding on a suffix beginning with a consonant.

EXAMPLES:

forget + **ing** ────▶ forgetting

commit + **al** ────▶ committal

equip + **ed** ────▶ equipped

but

forget + **ful** ────▶ forgetful

commit + **ment** ────▶ commitment

equip + **ment** ────▶ equipment

This rule is quite difficult to master as it relies on your ability to hear where the stress falls in a word. If you don't achieve success at first, don't despair. Be aware of the rule and use your dictionary to check if you are uncertain. You may even find that you don't need to remember the rule as you can tell by looking at the word whether it is correct.

** Look at these words and choose the correct spelling from each pair.

admited/admitted	filtered/filterred
begining/beginning	gossiped/gossipped
benefitted/benefited	gardener/gardenner
regretful/regrettful	piloted/pilotted
profitable/profittable	difference/differrence
submitted/submited	riveting/rivetting
transmitted/transmited	fidgetted/fidgeted

The 'l' rule

This rule is easy to apply. You may be able to work it out for yourself. Can you see what happens to these two-syllable words when a vowel suffix is added?

sig/nal becomes signalled

pat/rol becomes patrolling

ex/pel becomes expelled

la/bel becomes labelling

trav/el becomes traveller

but

ap/peal becomes appealing

con/ceal becomes concealed

If there is one vowel before 'l', double the 'l' when adding a vowel suffix.

If there are two vowels before 'l', don't double the 'l' when adding a vowel suffix.

Look at these words where a consonant suffix has been added.

quarrel becomes quarrelsome

fulfil becomes fulfilment

When a consonant suffix is added the 'l' is not doubled.

In two-syllable words which end in 'l' and have one vowel before the 'l', double the 'l' when adding a vowel suffix but don't double the 'l' when adding a consonant suffix.

There are a few exceptions to this rule:

formal + ity ⟶ formality

brutal + ity ⟶ brutality

civil + ity ⟶ civility

legal + ity ⟶ legality

civil + ise ⟶ civilise

legal + ise ⟶ legalise

Suffixing rules are useful as they help you to tackle a large number of words but if you find the rules difficult to remember, concentrate on other techniques to learn the spelling of the words to which the rules apply.

Tackle one rule at a time, test it out and use it. Find other words for which the rule works. Seeing the rule in practice will help you to understand and appreciate its usefulness.

13
The 'c' and 'g' Sounds

By now you are well aware of the fact that most letters in the alphabet can make different sounds in different words.

Hard and soft 'c'

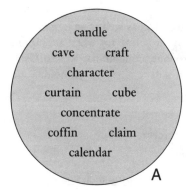

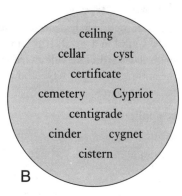

candle	ceiling
cave craft	cellar cyst
character	certificate
curtain cube	cemetery Cypriot
concentrate	centigrade
coffin claim	cinder cygnet
calendar	cistern
A	**B**

Read aloud the words in circle A and then circle B.

What is the difference in sound between the words in circles A and B?

All the words in circle A start with a hard 'c' sound (the same sound as 'k' makes) whereas the words in circle B begin with a soft 'c' sound (like the sound of the letter 's').

Hard and soft 'c' sounds can also occur in the middle of words.

list A	list B
tractor	recipe
bacon	spicy
acorn	place
document	recent
vocal	pacify

Study the words in circle B and list B and see if you can work out when 'c' is likely to make a soft sound. The clue lies in the letter following 'c'.

In all the words with a soft 'c' sound, the letter after 'c' is either e, i or y.

'c' usually makes an 's' sound when it is followed by 'e', 'i' or 'y'. Before the other vowels, 'a', 'o' 'u', and before consonants, 'c' will usually make a hard sound.

A soft 'c' is more usual in the middle and end of words than it is at the beginning.

In these words the soft 'c' sound occurs at the end.

policy	service	balance
urgency	confidence	office

Why is the rule helpful?

The soft 'c' rule helps you to understand that a 'c' as well as an 's' can make an 's' sound in a word. It is another option for you to try when attempting to spell a word. The rule helps you to pronounce unfamiliar words. Using the information you have about hard and soft 'c's, try to pronounce the following words.

centuplicate	cerebrospinal
calamus	campaniform
curvicaudate	covalency

word	meaning	pronunciation
centuplicate	one of a hundred like things or copies	The first 'c' is soft as it is followed by 'e'; the second 'c' is hard because it is followed by 'a'.
cerebrospinal	relating to the brain and spinal cord together	'c' is pronounced as an 's' sound as it is followed by 'e'.
calamus	a reed pen or quill	Here, a hard 'c' is needed as 'a' is the next letter.
campaniform	bell shaped	Again, 'c' is followed by 'a' so a hard sound is pronounced.

word	meaning	pronunciation
curvicaudate	having a crooked tail	Both 'c's will be hard sounds: the first is followed by 'u' and the second by 'a'.
covalency	union of two atoms sharing a pair of electrons	The first 'c' is pronounced as a hard sound because it precedes 'o'; the second 'c' will be an 's' sound as 'y' follows it.

Testing the soft 'c' rule

** Complete these words with 'c' or 's'.

lu_id	_ylinder	_aviour	pre_ise	con_eal
rea_on	_au_er	ac_ept	ex_ellent	pala_e
coun_il	par_el	con_entrate	_au_age	_urfa_e
curren_y	ne_essary	soli_itor	emergen_y	electri_ity

**Complete these words.

1 The twelfth month of the year   D_ _ _ _ _ _ _

2 Not guilty   i_ _ _ _ _ _ _

3 Taken when ill   m_ _ _ _ _ _ _

4 A letter ending 'Yours . . .'   s_ _ _ _ _ _ _

5 Hide   c_ _ _ _ _ _

6 To make up one's mind   d_ _ _ _ _

7 An ocean   P_ _ _ _ _ _

8 A performance of poetry or music   r_ _ _ _ _ _

9 Films are shown here   c_ _ _ _ _

10 This show sometimes has performing animals   c_ _ _ _ _

Problem words

cc

In some words where two 'c's occur together, the first 'c' makes a hard sound and the second a soft sound.

Section 3

13

hard 'c' sound

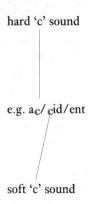

e.g. ac/ cid/ent

soft 'c' sound

** Divide these words into syllables then say each word aloud, listening for the hard 'c' at the end of the first syllable and the soft 'c' at the beginning of the second syllable.

accent	accept	accelerate
vaccination	eccentric	access

xc

EXAMPLES:

exceed	excellent	except
excel	excitement	excess

These words can sometimes cause problems as the 'x' and 'c' tend to go together to make an 's' sound. If you have difficulties with these words, exaggerate their pronunciation so that you hear both the 'x' and soft 'c'.

Retaining the 'e'

noticeable	traceable	peaceable
serviceable	irreplaceable	pronounceable

You may remember that these words are exceptions to the rule you learnt in Chapter 12. The 'e' is usually dropped when a vowel suffix is added but if the 'e' were omitted the words would be pronounced with a hard 'c' or 'k' sound. The 'e' is needed after 'c' so that 'c' can be pronounced as a soft sound.

Problem endings

Both 'ce' and 'se' are possible letter combinations when an 's' sound is needed at the end of a word, but 'ce' is more common than 'se'. As these two endings have the same sound, problems can arise.

ce	se
slice	cease
circumference	nonsense
experience	promise
difference	expense
pence	loose
conscience	chase
service	false
absence	tense
choice	increase
police	else

Helpful Hints

▶ Concentrate on the visual shape of the word and notice the 'ce' or 'se' at the end.

▶ If certain 'ce' or 'se' words cause problems, group them together and devise a mnemonic for them.

e.g. A false promise is nonsense.

noun	verb
practice	practise
licence	license
advice	advise
device	devise

▶ The words above can occur with 'ce' or 'se' at the end according to the way they are used in a sentence. Practice/practise and licence/license cause more confusion than the other two word pairs as the endings 'ise' and 'ice' are pronounced in exactly the same way. A slight difference in sound can be heard in the word endings of the other examples.

To help differentiate between the two endings, look at the   sentences overleaf.

Section 3

13

The football **practice** was held at the local recreation ground.

Here 'practice' is a noun (a naming word).

He must **practise** the piano each day if he is to improve.

Here 'practise' is a verb (an action word).

The same rule applies to the other words in the group.

The noun is spelt with 'c', the verb is spelt with 's'.

** Test the rule by choosing the correct word from the brackets for each of these sentences.

1 The policeman asked to see the motorist's driving (licence/license).

2 His employer asked him to put his ideas into (practice/practise).

3 I cannot drive my car until I (licence/license) it.

4 The teenage girl always ignored her mother's (advice/advise).

5 Every evening Clare had to (practice/practise) her part in the play.

6 He hoped that his latest (device/devise) would eventually be manufactured.

7 "I strongly (advice/advise) you not to enter the competition."

8 I frequently (device/devise) ideas for improving efficiency at the office.

Some 'ce' words have an 'i' before them and so end in the word 'ice'.

EXAMPLES:

notice	voice	juice
twice	office	price

Noticing the familiar word at the end and exaggerating its pronunciation may help you remember its spelling.

Other 'ce' words end in the word 'ace'.

EXAMPLES:

palace	space	trace
grace	place	race

Exaggerate the 'ace' part of the word when pronouncing it, to help you remember the spelling.

guarantee
gyrate   gist
giraffe
game   ghost
granite
general   gentry
gutter
gentle   genius
geography
great   glaze
gesture

**Sort these words into two groups:

those beginning with a hard 'g' and

those beginning with a soft 'g'.

Hard and soft 'g'

Look carefully at the words in your soft 'g' group. Which letters occur after a soft 'g'?

Like 'c', 'g' often makes a soft sound if followed by 'e', 'i' or 'y'. When it is followed by the vowels, 'a', 'o', 'u', or consonants, it generally makes a hard sound.

Soft 'g' at the beginning of words

The soft 'g' rule is not as reliable as the soft 'c' rule at the beginning of words, as there are a number of quite common words in which 'g' followed by 'e', 'i' or 'y' has a hard sound.

13

EXAMPLES:

get	give	gear	gift	giddy
geese	giggle	girl	girdle	geyser

Soft 'g' in the middle of words

Like soft 'c', soft 'g' is present in the middle of words and here it is much more consistent in the sound it makes.

EXAMPLES:

magic	engineer	urgent	agile	imagination
apologise	engine	suggest	margin	emergency

Helpful Hints

▶ 'g' in such words as 'forgive', 'target' and 'forget' will have a hard sound based on the words 'give' and 'get'.

▶ 'g' in 'begin' is a hard sound.

▶ In 'gadget', 'midget' 'budget' and 'fidget' the 'g' of 'get' is soft.

Soft 'g' at the end of words

You read in Chapter 6 that no English word ends in 'j'. When a 'j' sound is heard at the end of words it is made by 'ge' or 'dge'.

EXAMPLES:

forge	storage	engage	carriage	porridge
hedge	college	emerge	badge	wage

In words ending with 'dge' the 'd' is silent.

A 'jee' sound at the end of words is made by 'gy'.

EXAMPLES:

dingy	stingy	biology	apology

In such words 'g' has a soft sound as it is followed by 'y'.

Some 'ge' words have an 'a' before the final 'ge'.

EXAMPLES:

savage	damage	bandage
manage	cabbage	postage

Seeing the word 'age' and exaggerating its pronunciation can help you recall its spelling.

Testing the soft 'g' rule

**Enter the missing letters.

g_psy	g_mnasium	charg_
g_ng_r	hing_	mer_ _
neglig_nt	g_neration	trag_c
oxyg_n	dredg_	pag_ant
barrag_	gara_ _	ag_ncy

**Complete the crossword grid.

Across 1   A military rank (8)
         3   A precious stone (3)
         5   Contains all the names of the class (8)
         7   A cause of disease (4)
         9   Not false (7)
Down   2   A language (7)
         4   A wedding (8)
         6   A doctor's consulting room (7)
         8   An annoying insect (5)

13

Problem words

| outrageous | knowledgeable | exchangeable |
| manageable | courageous | advantageous |

All these words seem to disobey the suffixing rule given in Chapter 12. The 'e' has to be kept before the vowel suffix to stop the 'g' making a hard sound.

**Refer to the rules outlined in this chapter then use your dictionary to see if you can find other words as examples of each guideline. Remember these are only guidelines and there will be exceptions so note down the exceptions as well. Use the dictionary's pronunciation guide so that you can see whether a 'c' or 'g' is soft or hard.

The more you learn about the language, the easier spelling becomes.

14
'i' before 'e'

The order in which 'i' and 'e' occur in words often causes a problem for the speller. 'i' before 'e' except after 'c' is the widely known rule for dealing with this problem.

Does the rule work?

EXAMPLES:

freight	leisure
deign	deceive

It is an excellent rule if you know the *complete* rule:

'i' before 'e' except after 'c' but only in words where these letters make an ē sound.

Read these words aloud.

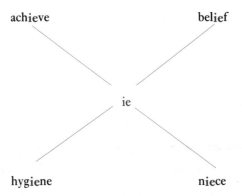

achieve   belief

ie

hygiene   niece

In each of the words there is an ē sound, so 'i' comes before 'e'.

There is also an ē sound in these words:

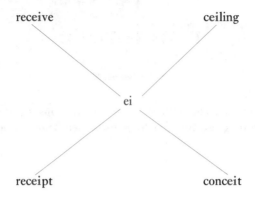

here 'e' comes before 'i' as the letter combination comes after 'c'.

Read these words.

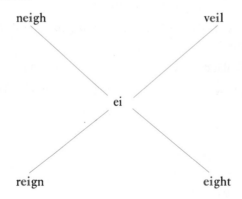

What vowel sound do you hear?

ā is heard so the spelling follows the rule: 'ei' if not an ē sound.

As you can hear, 'reign' has an ā sound and an 'ei' spelling.

reign

foreign

sovereign

Whether you hear an ā sound in 'foreign' and 'sovereign' may depend on your accent, but remember the 'ei' spelling of the 'reign' family.

Testing the 'i' before 'e' rule
**Complete each word with 'ie' or 'ei'.

d_ _sel	conc_ _ve	w_ _ght
fr_ _ght	shr_ _k	perc_ _ve
th_ _f	ach_ _ve	rel_ _f
n_ _ghbour	v_ _n	f_ _ld
br_ _f	dec_ _ve	gr_ _ve
dec_ _t	bes_ _ge	pr_ _st
p_ _ce	retr_ _ve	ch_ _f

Other 'ei' words
'ei' doesn't always make an ā sound.

EXAMPLES:

heifer
leisure ĕ

height ——— ī

weir
weird 'ear'

heir
heiress 'air'
their

Nevertheless, these words obey the 'i' before 'e' rule as they don't contain an ē sound.

Real exceptions
counterfeit

protein
caffeine

seize

You may find it helpful to learn the exceptions by devising a memorable sentence for them, such as

He seized the counterfeit protein and caffeine.

either and neither
You may or may not pronounce these with a long ē sound, depending on your preference. However, they must be spelled 'ei'.

14

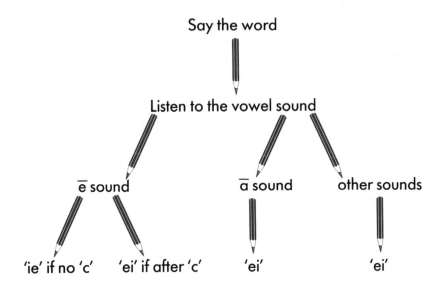

Say the word

Listen to the vowel sound

ē sound   ā sound   other sounds

'ie' if no 'c'   'ei' if after 'c'   'ei'   'ei'

Other 'ie' combinations

There are other instances when 'i' and 'e' occur together and there is no ē sound.

▶ When there are two separate sounds
▶ In 'y' rule words
▶ In 'ci' words

When there are two separate sounds
EXAMPLES:

audience	au/di/ence
alien	a/li/en
society	so/ci/et/y
science	sci/ence
convenient	con/ve/ni/ent
experience	ex/per/i/ence

Generally there are fewer problems with such words because you can hear 'i' and 'e' making separate sounds when you divide each word into syllables.

In 'y' rule words

EXAMPLES:

reply ———— replies
          ———— replied

tiny ———— tiniest
         ———— tinier

defy ———— defies
         ———— defied

In Chapter 12 you were shown that when most suffixes are added to words ending in a consonant and 'y', the 'y' changes to an 'i'. By recognising the pattern, you will have no difficulty with the order of 'i' and 'e' in such words.

In 'ci' words

EXAMPLES:

sufficient	efficient
deficient	proficient
ancient	conscience

In words where 'ci' produces a 'sh' sound, 'i' comes before 'e'.

Other 'sh' words

The 'sh' sound can cause spelling difficulties because 'si', 'ci', 'ti' and 'xi' can all make a 'sh' sound.

EXAMPLES:

si	ci	ti	xi
controversial	official	essential	complexion
	artificial	partial	anxious
	suspicious	influential	
	politician	confidential	
		ambitious	

14

**Complete these words, using 'ci' or 'ti' in each case.

torren_ _al	spe_ _al	spa_ _ous
pa_ _ent	vi_ _ous	infec_ _ous
so_ _ally	pre_ _ous	cons_ _ous
deli_ _ous	ficti_ _ous	finan_ _al
opti_ _an	appre_ _ate	electri_ _an

15
Informed Choice

This chapter deals with homophones.

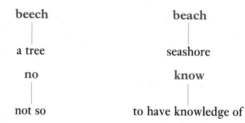

homophone

'same'   'sound'

Homophones are words which sound the same but are spelt differently and have different meanings.

EXAMPLES:

beech	beach
a tree	seashore
no	know
not so	to have knowledge of

As pairs of homophones share the same sound, there can be confusion about which one to use. In this chapter you will be given

▶ examples of homophones

▶ guidance on meaning and usage

▶ hints and strategies for remembering the right word in the right context

Everyday errors

These words are frequently used but can still present problems.

two, to and too

its and it's

here and hear

there, their and they're

your and you're

whose and who's

passed and past

Section 3

15

Tackle one group at a time and learn it thoroughly before working on another group. Follow these steps with each group.

Concentrate on one word
and its meaning.

|

Learn each other word in
the group in the same way.

|

Test your knowledge.

|

Can you choose the right
word for the situation?

If you have difficulty with one of the groups, follow the path below.

Make yourself aware of
how the words are used.

|

Look in newspapers and magazines
for the words.

|

Highlight the word/s.

|

What does it mean
in this sentence?

|

Use the word in a
sentence of your own.

|

Keep practising!

If you are uncertain about a particular homophone when you are writing, underline the word and check it when you have completed your writing.

Be aware of possible errors in using homophones when you proof-read your writing.

two, to, and too

▶ **two** is always used for the number 2.

e.g. There were two people in the shop.

▶ **to** has two uses:

to show the direction 'towards';

e.g. The passengers were all travelling to Edinburgh.

and with a verb to form the infinitive.

e.g. The lift was designed **to carry** five people.

$$\downarrow$$

infinitive

▶ **too** also has two meanings:

'as well' or 'also';

e.g. When I am in France, I shall visit Paris too.

or 'excess' (too much).

e.g. It was too hot for comfort. (excess heat)

Helpful Hints

▶ **two** rarely presents difficulties and is easy to remember.

▶ **to** is the most frequently used word of the group.

▶ **too** is the one that can present the most difficulty. You could try thinking of it as

one 'o' <u>as well as</u> another 'o' (meaning 'as well' or 'also'), or

<u>too many</u> 'o's (meaning 'excess').

** Complete this passage with **to**, **two** or **too**.

It was ...... dark ...... see the buildings which surrounded him but the faint sound of the motorway traffic made him realise that he had gone ...... far. He had hoped ...... be near the river. However, it seemed that, although he had been walking for ...... hours, he wasn't going ...... reach his destination yet. He was tired, and hungry .... Impatience made him break into a run. He was willing ...... risk being heard, if he could get ...... the mooring in time.

its and it's

Look at these two sentences:

The dog yelped as the vet gently lifted its paw.

It's a beautiful day.

What's the difference in use between **its** and **it's**?

In the first sentence above, 'its paw' refers to the paw belonging to the dog. **Its always means 'belonging to it'.**

In the second sentence, **it's** is a shortened form of 'it is'. **It's stands for 'it is' or 'it has'.**

The apostrophe shows that the letter 'i' of 'is' or the letters 'ha' of 'has' have been omitted.

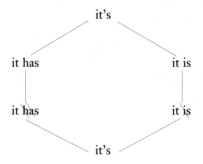

▶ When using either of these spellings, think of the meaning carefully; you can quite easily work out which to use.

▶ If you can replace the word with 'it is' or 'it has', then **it's** is the spelling you need.

** Use its or it's in each of these sentences.

1 .... been a long time.

2 The company announced an increase in ...... profits.

3 The cat opened ...... eyes and stretched.

4 If ...... too hot, leave it until it cools down.

5 I don't like to be too inquisitive but ...... very puzzling.

6 The shop will be closing ...... doors in a few minutes.

7 .... no wonder he failed his driving test.

8 He doesn't like the car because ...... too small.

9 The roof leaks when ...... raining.

10 .... tyres look quite worn.

here and hear

▶ here means 'in this place'.

   e.g. The book is here.

▶ hear means the action of hearing.

   e.g. I can hear his footsteps.

▶ Remember the meaning of 'hear' by the sentence 'We hear with our ears'.

▶ Link 'here' with the other 'place' words in the phrase 'here, there and everywhere'.

Section 3

15

there, their and they're

▶ **there** has two uses. It shows place

e.g. The car was parked there. (position)

and is used with the verb 'to be'.

e.g. There have been many accidents on that stretch of road.

(Remember: 'there is' and 'there has' are often shortened in informal writing to **there's**.)

▶ **their** means 'belonging to them'.

e.g. This is their car.

▶ **they're** is the shortened form of 'they are'.

e.g. They're often away at this time of year.

Helpful Hints

▶ **they're** is the easiest to use in a sentence. It can always be replaced with 'they are'.

▶ Try **their** next. Look at the sentence. Do they 'own' something?

▶ Remember 'here, **there** and everywhere' are all 'place' words.

Testing yourself

** Complete this conversation with **here, hear, there, their, they're, it's, its, to, two** or **too**.

MYRA   .... is the cinema. I said it was over ....

TONY   .... is an enormous queue. I think ...... all waiting

for the film on screen .... I can ...... the

manager shouting that ...... are only twenty seats left.

MYRA   Shall we wait .... or go round and see Mike and John?

TONY   We could go round to ...... house.

...... not ...... far from ...... and I know ......

usually at home on a Thursday evening.

your and you're

Compare these two sentences.

"Is that **your** hammer?"

"**You're** always late."

▶ your means 'belonging to you'.

▶ you're is the shortened form of 'you are'.

Helpful Hints

▶ If the word you have written can be replaced by 'you are', then **you're** is needed.

whose and who's

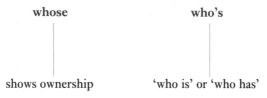

whose   who's

shows ownership   'who is' or 'who has'

EXAMPLES:

This is the man who's going to be our foreman. (**Who's** can be replaced by 'who is'.)

I'm not sure whose dog it is. (Replacing **whose** with 'who is' would not make sense.)

passed and past

This is probably the most difficult pair of homophones in the group.

▶ **passed** has several meanings:

'went by',

e.g. He passed the shop on his way to work.

'transferred',

e.g. She passed the plate to him.

'got through',

e.g. I passed all my examinations last summer.

and 'met with acceptance'.

e.g. The council passed the plans after a vote.

15

▶ **past** is also used in several different ways:

to tell the time,

e.g. It is half-past eight.

to mean 'beyond' or 'by',

e.g. We walked past the stadium.

and to mean 'bygone'.

e.g. He belongs to a past generation.

Helpful Hints

▶ Test for 'passed'. If it doesn't work, use 'past'.

The two-step test for 'passed'

▶ **passed** is a verb (a word of action).

▶ In front of any verb you can place one of these words: I, you, he, she, it, we or they.

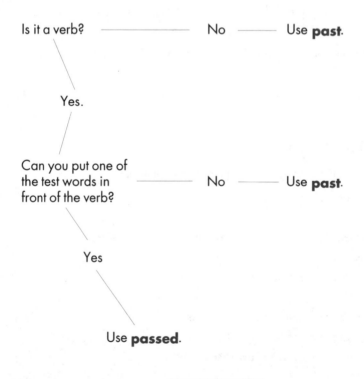

Is it a verb? ——————— No ——— Use **past**.

\
　Yes.
　/
Can you put one of
the test words in ——————— No ——— Use **past**.
front of the verb?
　\
　　Yes
　　\
　　　Use **passed**.

** Use 'passed' or 'past' correctly in each of these sentences.

1 The car sped ...... the finish at 150 mph.

2 The car looks ...... its best.

3 Mrs Redwood ...... the message on to the manager.

4 It's ...... his bedtime.

5 His ...... career was remarkable.

6 In spite of all their fears, she ...... the examination.

7 The house is just ...... the library.

8 We will forget about the ....

9 The car ...... its MOT.

10 She remembered her ...... mistakes.

Common homophones

As you saw in Chapters 9 and 10, there are often several ways of spelling a sound.

e.g. The sound ā can be spelt 'a-e', 'ai' or 'ay'.

It is because of these alternative ways of spelling sounds that we have many of our homophones.

EXAMPLES:

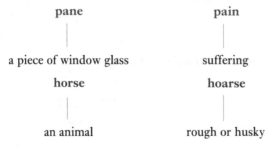

Sometimes mistakes occur because the speller is only aware of one spelling and believes that it is suitable for all the meanings of the word.

15

** Find another word which sounds exactly the same as each of these.

e.g. cruise and crews

miner	morning	steal
story	board	grown
hall	peer	pair
caught	altar	shoot
style	allowed	hire

When you have checked your answers, you may need to use a dictionary to check the meanings of some of the words.

** Complete the second word in each of these pairs of homophones.

stair and st _ _ e	mind and mi_ _d
shore and s _ _ e	muscle and mu_ _ _l
air and _ _ir	lesson and les_ _n
ceiling and _ _aling	stayed and st_ _d
metal and me _ _ _e	piece and p_ _ _e
hour and _ _r	navel and n_ _ _l

**Look at the following groups of homophones and check the meaning of any unfamiliar words in a dictionary. Try to be aware of their different meanings when you use them in your writing.

sent and scent	real and reel	lone and loan
new and knew	tale and tail	none and nun
weight and wait		peel and peal
one and won	vale and veil	plum and plumb
pale and pail	peak and peek	tears and tiers

paw, pour and pore	sight, site and cite
vain, vane and vein	pear, pair and pare
for, four and fore	saw, sore and soar

** Find the pair of homophones to match the clues given below.

e.g.   a metal   _steel_

       to take illegally   _steal_

1 A part of a church   _____

  An area of land surrounded by water   _____

2 A vault   _____

  A vendor   _____

3 A discovery   _____

  Made to pay a penalty   _____

4 Used to measure the value of gold and diamonds   _____

  A vegetable   _____

5 Caused by a burst pipe   _____

  Popular with Welsh people   _____

6 Rubbish?   _____

  This measurement often causes concern   _____

7 Film or pop star?   _____

  Lazy   _____

8 Payment for a journey   _____

  Reasonable   _____

9 Smaller than a raisin   _____

  Happening now   _____

10 To caution someone   _____

   Showing the effects of age   _____

15

Special homophones

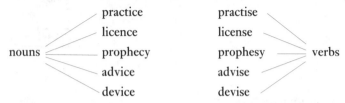

nouns	practice	practise
	licence	license
	prophecy	prophesy	verbs
	advice	advise
	device	devise

Chapter 13 dealt with these special homophones, and gave the rule: **the noun is spelt with 'c', the verb with 's'.**

The last two pairs are the easiest to work out as you can hear a difference between the two spellings:

> **advice** and **device** rhyme with 'ice';

> **advise** and **devise** rhyme with 'ize'.

Use the noun/verb rule to distinguish between the other pairs of words.

If you are uncertain about their use, look back to Chapter 13.

More difficult homophones

e.g.   **canvas**   **canvass**

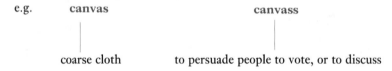

coarse cloth   to persuade people to vote, or to discuss

Memory aids

As the homophones introduced here are perhaps less obvious and less frequently used, it may be necessary to devise techniques to help you recall them.

▶ Remember the shape of the word. Concentrate on the difference between how the two words look. (e.g. the 'ss' of 'canvass'.)

▶ Make up a mnemonic.

EXAMPLES:

A 'gorilla' is a kind of ape.   A 'guerilla' war is waged by a small band of fighters who harass a larger army.

See the urban enemy in guerilla.

To 'assent' is to agree.   An 'ascent' is a climb.

Say 'yes' to assent.   Climb the ascent.

▶ Look for a word within one of the pair which will help you recall its spelling.

e.g. 'Serial' means forming a series; 'cereal' is a grain or a breakfast food.

I eat real cereals

▶ Adapt the pronunciation.

e.g. 'lightening' means to make lighter; 'lightning' is the electric flash which precedes thunder.

Stress the 'ten' in 'lightening' to differentiate between the two words.

** Complete each of the sentences below with one of the words from these pairs.

forth	fourth	course	coarse
taught	taut	prize	prise
dependent	dependant	compliment	complement
horde	hoard	waive	wave
counsellor	councillor	sheer	shear

1 Help me to ...... this lid off.

2 He kept a ...... of tinned food in his cupboard.

3 The accused intends to ...... his right to speak.

4 There was a ...... drop below them.

15

5 The mooring rope was pulled ...... in the gale.

6 The ...... won the local election.

7 You can claim tax relief if she is your ....

8 The teacher had a reputation for being ...... right.

9 The race ...... measured two miles.

10 Most people enjoy receiving a ...... about their appearance.

Homophones can create dilemmas but, by being aware of their existence and carefully considering their meanings, you will find it possible to make an informed choice. Chapter 18 provides examples of other confusing words and guidance on their use.

16
Word Endings

A stress problem

When we speak, we put emphasis on a certain part of each word. This stress pattern was acquired quite naturally when we learnt to speak. Stress gives language its rhythm and range of intonation.

If you say these words aloud you may be able to hear where the emphasis lies.

<u>ru</u>stle	att<u>ack</u>	ma<u>te</u>rial
<u>es</u>tuary	<u>hap</u>py	<u>mess</u>age

The stressed part of each word is underlined.

When you look up the meaning of an unfamiliar word in a dictionary you are shown where the emphasis should be placed.

In the majority of words the stress is placed on the first part, making this syllable seem slightly louder than the rest of the word. Consequently the voice trails off at the end of the word making the unstressed final syllable difficult to hear. This often causes the final syllable to be spelt incorrectly, especially in longer words.

A variety of endings

Although the problem of endings has already been highlighted in Chapters 5 and 12, in this chapter you will be shown other endings and given guidelines and advice to help overcome any possible spelling difficulties.

This chapter is a reference section for word endings, so dip into it and concentrate on one group of endings at a time.

Section 3

16

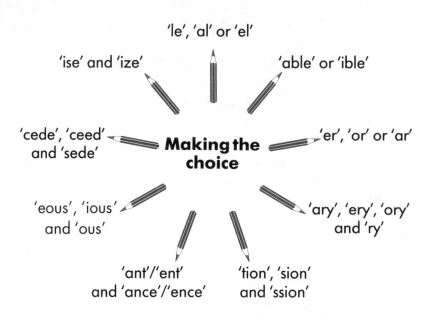

'le', 'al' or 'el'

'ise' and 'ize'

'able' or 'ible'

'cede', 'ceed' and 'sede'

Making the choice

'er', 'or' or 'ar'

'eous', 'ious' and 'ous'

'ary', 'ery', 'ory' and 'ry'

'ant'/'ent' and 'ance'/'ence'

'tion', 'sion' and 'ssion'

'le', 'al' or 'el'

EXAMPLES:

people   channel   petal

The ending of each word shown above sounds the same but the sound is made by different vowels combining with 'l'.

The ending 'ol' can also make the same sound (e.g. 'idol') but it appears in very few words.

There are some guidelines that you can follow in order to make an informed choice but the guidelines are wordy and there are exceptions.

'le' guidelines

table	article	candle	rifle	struggle
sparkle	treacle	example	settle	puzzle

▶ The 'c' in 'treacle' and 'article' and 'g' in 'struggle' are hard sounds because they are followed by 'l'. If 'c' or 'g' is soft, it cannot be followed by 'le' or 'al': el must be used.

EXAMPLES:

angel

parcel

▶ Words with a hard 'c' before the final 'ul' sound are easier to deal with as there are firm guidelines.

cal	cle
musical	miracle
critical	icicle
classical	circle
magical	vehicle
physical	cubicle

The choice between 'cal' and 'cle' as an ending depends on the way the word is used.

The 'cal' words are adjectives (describing words); 'cle' words are nouns (naming words).

e.g. The clergyman never wore his clerical collar unless he was conducting a service.

adjective (describes the collar)

e.g. He is prepared to overcome any obstacle in order to achieve his ambition.

noun

▶ There are certain combinations of letters which do not occur in English: 'mle', 'nle', 'rle', 'vle' and 'wle'.

'el' guidelines

cancel	angel	camel	tunnel	quarrel
shrivel	panel	towel	jewel	gravel

▶ As 'mle', 'nle', 'rle', 'vle' and 'wle' are not acceptable English endings, the 'ul' sound after 'm', 'n', 'r', 'v', and 'w' can only be made by el or al.

▶ After soft 'c' and 'g' the 'ul' ending will be made by el.

▶ There are words which end in el to which no guidelines can be applied.

16

EXAMPLES:

rebel	expel	fuel	parallel	vessel
label	chapel	cruel	model	chisel

'al' guidelines

hospital	metal	approval	proposal	special
rehearsal	signal	several	material	removal

As there are no reliable guidelines, make up mnemonics for groups of 'al' words that repeatedly present problems for you.

Helpful Hints

▶ If you think that a word you have written looks wrong, try an alternative 'ul' sounding ending.

▶ When you cannot judge from its visual appearance whether it is right or wrong, use your dictionary. It is fairly easy to look up a word when you are uncertain of its ending as you already have the main part of the word worked out.

▶ Try to exaggerate the ending when you pronounce the word in order to spell it. This isn't easy with 'le' words but it is more possible with 'el' and 'al' endings.

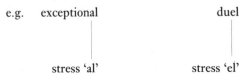

e.g.   exceptional   duel

            stress 'al'   stress 'el'

Using the guidelines

** Spell these words correctly by choosing the correct ending, 'al', 'el' or 'le' in each case.

stab_ _	dent_ _	ment_ _
coast_ _	responsib_ _	vegetab_ _
fat_ _	terrib_ _	nav_ _
scand_ _	sand_ _	cryst_ _
reb_ _	rust_ _	sing_ _

'able' or 'ible'

able	ible
lovable	visible
valuable	possible
changeable	incredible
understandable	irresistible
flammable	reversible
movable	flexible

The 'able' and 'ible' suffixes both sound the same and mean 'being fit or able to'.

e.g. 'visible' means something which can be seen.

There is no foolproof way of knowing which ending to choose.

Guidelines

▶ able is more common than ible.

▶ When the base word is kept and not altered, it is usual to add able.

EXAMPLES:

reason becomes reasonable

impression becomes impressionable

commend becomes commendable

depend becomes dependable

▶ Words ending in 'able' and 'ible' are adjectives (describing words). Words ending in 'ation' are nouns (naming words). Most nouns ending in ation become able when an adjective is formed.

e.g.   consider<u>ation</u>   dur<u>ation</u>

         consider<u>able</u>   dur<u>able</u>

▶ When adding able and ible to words ending in a silent 'e', remove the 'e' before adding the suffix.

EXAMPLES:

admire becomes admirable

force becomes forcible

sense becomes sensible

16

▶ Words with a soft 'c' or 'g' retain the final 'e' before adding the suffix so that the 'c' or 'g' can remain as a soft sound.

e.g.   noticeable   manageable

▶ able forms a word in its own right and ible is an easy group of letters to pronounce as a unit, so try stressing the pronunciation of the ending of the word as you write it.

EXAMPLES:

desirable   irresponsible

objectionable   compatible

justifiable   horrible

▶ If you have difficulty remembering particular words, group them into a mnemonic.

e.g. He is a valuable, capable and dependable worker.

** Using the guidelines.

Complete the passage using 'able' or 'ible'.

His unmistak_ _ _ _ ability as a musician is instantly

recognis_ _ _ _ and it is inevit_ _ _ _ that he will

eventually become famous. By nature he is soci_ _ _ _,

hospit_ _ _ _, excit_ _ _ _, change_ _ _ _ and at times even

miser_ _ _ _. The press always remarks upon his

fashion _ _ _ _ clothes and his terr_ _ _ _ temper.

** Make these nouns into adjectives ending in 'able' or 'ible'.

e.g. negotiation becomes negotiable.

justification	inflammation	objection	adoration
irritation	reputation	navigation	commendation
application	variation	admiration	estimation

'er', 'or' or 'ar'

In Chapter 10 you read about 'er', 'ur' and 'ir' all making an 'er' sound. Here we will consider words ending in an 'er' sound. At the end of words this sound is usually made by 'er', 'or' or, less frequently, 'ar'. Such endings pose a dilemma for many people when they write as there are no hard and fast rules, but knowledge of the guidelines can help as long as you remember that not all words neatly fit into them and there will be exceptions. When you are uncertain, you can always consult your dictionary.

'er' guidelines

▶ Words with a soft 'c' or 'g' sound will naturally need an er ending to keep the 'c' or 'g' soft.

EXAMPLES:

officer	manager	grocer
ranger	tracer	exchanger

▶ Some verbs which end in a silent 'e' become nouns ending in er. Such verbs tend to be short and simple.

EXAMPLES:

bake/baker	write/writer
make/maker	gamble/gambler
dine/diner	observe/observer
mine/miner	poke/poker

▶ The er sound in all these words for relations is spelt er: brother, sister, mother, father and daughter.

▶ The most usual way of ending a word which describes someone carrying out an action is er.

action	person carrying out the action
farming	farmer
cleaning	cleaner
gardening	gardener
robbing	robber
performing	performer
photographing	photographer

'or' guidelines

When the base word ends in

    ate

    ct

    it

    ession

the 'er' sound is spelt or.

ate	it
accelerator (accelerate)	editor (edit)
excavator (excavate)	visitor (visit)
operator (operate)	solicitor (solicit)

ct	ession
actor (act)	professor (profession)
director (direct)	successor (succession)
collector (collect)	confessor (confession)

This is a very reliable guideline.

'ar' guidelines

vicar	altar	popular	familiar	beggar
burglar	grammar	similar	peculiar	collar

For words ending in ar there are no guidelines and these may be learnt:

> visually;

> by exaggerating the 'ar' ending;

> by grouping words together and forming mnemonics.

▶ our also makes an 'er' sound at the ends of words.

EXAMPLES:

flavour	neighbour	rumour	parlour
armour	vapour	harbour	labour
honour	humour	colour	favour

Again there are no guidelines to help you make the right choice. In American spelling the ending of such words is spelt 'or'.

▶ There are two other endings that make an 'er' sound at the ends of words: a and re.

a	re
camera	centre
arena	acre
trauma	theatre

As they are less common endings they can be learnt as they present themselves in your writing.

** Applying the guidelines

Arrange these words in groups according to the ending of the base word. The endings are: 'ate', 'ct', 'it' and 'ession'.

instructor	creditor
calculator	inspector
inheritor	dictator
creator	elector
radiator	possessor

** Find appropriate 'or', 'er' or 'ar' endings for these base words. The guidelines will help you with some of them but for others you may need to use your dictionary to check.

select	compute	survive	invent
play	conquer	supervise	distribute
survey	desert	compete	err
travel	council	fertilise	custom

'ary', 'ery', 'ory' and 'ry'

EXAMPLES:

library	bakery	compulsory	poetry
dictionary	robbery	directory	cavalry

All these words sound as if they end in 'ree'. In the 'ary', 'ery' and 'ory' endings the vowels are swallowed up as our voices trail off towards the end of the words. Such endings can cause confusion even for people who consider themselves to be good spellers. There are no rules to help with the dilemma, but the following guidelines may help.

Guidelines

▶ The guidelines that helped you choose the ending 'er' or 'or' can be applied here.

▶ A word which ends in 'ar', 'er', 'or' or 'ar' will usually retain a consistent pattern.

er	or	ar
brewer	supervisor	burglar
brewery	supervisory	burglary

▶ **ery** is usually *added* to a base word.

e.g. machine/machinery   nurse/nursery

▶ **ary** or **ory** can be an *essential part* of a base word but there is no way of distinguishing which words end in **ary** and which in **ory**.

Janu<u>ary</u>	st<u>ory</u>
Febru<u>ary</u>	fact<u>ory</u>
annivers<u>ary</u>	gl<u>ory</u>
secret<u>ary</u>	hist<u>ory</u>
gloss<u>ary</u>	dormit<u>ory</u>

▶ Stationary/stationery and accessary/accessory have two forms according to the way the words are used. It helps if you know the baseword.

station   stationer

stationary   stationery

to stand still at   e for the envelopes sold by
the station.   the stationer.

an accessary is a person who   an accessory is an ornament;
helps in a crime.   something extra but non-essential.

a for aids and abets.   o for ornament.

▶ **ury** can also make the same sound at the end of words but it is less common.

EXAMPLES:

century	injury
perjury	treasury

Again, use other techniques to help you. Probably the most useful way is to overstress and overpronounce the endings. Many words end in the word 'tory', as you can see from the list of 'ory' words, so concentrate on this word within a word.

Choosing endings

** Use your dictionary if necessary to complete these words with 'ary', 'ery' 'ory' and 'ry'.

cemet........	bound........
surg........	regist........
necess........	custom........
cook........	chival........
infant........	lavat........
discov........	ordin........
poult........	myst........
mem........	milit........

'tion', 'sion' and 'ssion'

EXAMPLES:

conversation	mansion	permission
nation	occasion	succession
relation	invasion	possession

If you read these words aloud, you will notice that each word ends in a 'shun' sound. There are other ways of making a 'shun' sound at the end of words

<u>cean</u>	<u>cian</u>	<u>cion</u>	<u>sian</u>
ocean	musician	suspicion	Asian

but these endings are less frequently used.

Guidelines

▶ When in doubt, use tion because the majority of words with a 'shun' sound at the end are spelt this way.

▶ In many of the ssion words, you will notice that the base word ends in 'ss'.

EXAMPLES:

discussion (discuss)	expression (express)
procession (process)	possession (possess)
repression (repress)	supression (supress)
succession (success)	impression (impress)

▶ Only cushion and fashion have the letters 'sh' at the beginning of the 'shun' syllable.

16

Test yourself

e.g. If you <u>examine</u> something, you carry out an <u>examination</u>.

verb   noun

Notice the final e of 'examine' is dropped when the vowel suffix is added.

e.g. If you <u>consider</u> a matter, you give it your <u>consideration</u>.

verb   noun

Sometimes an a is added before tion to make the word easier to say.

In some words the verb is altered before the suffix is added.

EXAMPLES:

permit becomes permission

provide becomes provision

** Turn these verbs into nouns.

omit	collide	profess	separate	destroy
invent	abolish	compete	decide	confuse
revise	televise	infect	compose	explode

'ant'/'ent' and 'ance'/'ence'

<u>ant</u>	<u>ent</u>
important	permanent
observant	confident
ignorant	imminent

It is difficult to hear any difference between the two endings ant and ent as the voice drops at the end of the word. The same thing happens with ance and ence words.

<u>ance</u>	<u>ence</u>
attendance	influence
grievance	correspondence
appearance	intelligence

Guidelines

Words that end in 'ent' generally take the suffix ence and those ending in 'ant' become ance

EXAMPLES:

relevance (relevant)	independence (independent)
abundance (abundant)	difference (different)
elegance (elegant)	convenience (convenient)

Helpful Hints

▶ As there are no set patterns, you need to use other techniques to tackle these endings.

▶ Probably the most effective way is to exaggerate the pronunciation of 'ent/ence' and 'ant/ance'.

▶ Certain words end in a recognisable word so identify and concentrate on it.

EXAMPLES:

rant in ignorant

dent in impudent

cent in innocent

fence in offence

dance in attendance

▶ Such words within words can be connected by mnemonics.

e.g. You might rant and rave if you are ignorant.

▶ Certain words alter their base spelling pattern when the suffix is added.

EXAMPLES:

maintenance (maintain)

remembrance (remember)

entrance (enter)

Sorting out the dilemma

** Devise techniques or memory aids to help you remember the spelling of these words which may cause you difficulties.

patient/patience	tenant	experience
obedient/obedience	vacant	apparent
innocent/innocence	extravagant	assistance
prominent/prominence	continent	circumstance
fragrant/fragrance	ornament	preference

Section 3

16

'eous', 'ious' and 'ous'

The ous suffix means 'full of'.

e.g. Cautious means full of caution.

EXAMPLES:

piteous	furious	marvellous
courageous	anxious	mountainous

Guidelines

▶ ous is added to words which end in a consonant.

EXAMPLES:

dangerous

prosperous

joyous

▶ As has already been said, words ending in a silent 'e' omit the 'e' before adding the vowel suffix ous.

EXAMPLES:

virtuous (virtue)

adventurous (adventure)

nervous (nerve)

▶ By now, you should be aware that after a soft 'c' or 'g' sound an 'e', 'i', or 'y' is needed to keep the letters soft.

When 'ous' is added to words with a soft 'c', an 'i' is substituted for the 'e'.

EXAMPLES:

gracious (grace)

spacious (space)

In the following words an 'e' or 'i' is retained after the 'g'.

EXAMPLES:

disadvantageous

outrageous

religious

▶ You are familiar with 'y' being replaced by 'i' before an ending is added. When ous is added to a word ending in 'y', there are two alternatives:

y becomes i and ous is added

or y becomes e and ous is added.

It is necessary to learn which words become eous and which ious.

ious	eous
glorious (glory)	piteous (pity)
industrious (industry)	plenteous (plenty)
furious (fury)	courteous (courtesy)

In both cases the 'i' and 'e' before the 'ous' ending have an ē sound.

▶ In some words ending in ious the 'ci' or 'ti' is pronounced as a 'sh' sound.

EXAMPLES:

| delicious | suspicious | precious |
| ambitious | vicious | officious |

▶ Words like humour, glamour and vigour change their spelling by dropping the 'u' when an ous ending is added.

humour becomes humorous

glamour becomes glamorous

vigour becomes vigorous

▶ You have already encountered words ending in 'f' where 'f' changes to 'v' when a plural ending is added. When ous is added to words ending in 'f', the f becomes v.

EXAMPLES:

mischief becomes mischievous

grief becomes grievous

Section 3

Helpful Hints

It is not possible to exaggerate the pronunciation of these endings in order to spell them, so:

concentrate on the visual aspect of each word

check the word you want to spell against the guidelines

group words sharing the same ending together.

16

Trying out the guidelines

** Use 'eous', 'ious' or 'ous' to form words with 'ous' sounding endings.

study	curiosity
mystery	glory
conscience	adventure
grace	religion
space	humour

'cede', 'ceed' and 'sede'

EXAMPLES:

precede   proceed   supersede

All three letter combinations sound the same but are fairly easy to deal with as few words have such endings.

Guidelines

▶ Most words end in 'cede'.

EXAMPLES:

recede   accede   intercede

▶ Learn the 'ceed' exceptions.

    proceed

    exceed

    succeed

Perhaps a mnemonic will help.

e.g. If I proceed, I will succeed and exceed my expectations.

▶ The only word to end in 'sede' is supersede.

'ise' and 'ize'

People often have a personal preference for one of these endings: Americans prefer 'ize'. Newspapers and publishers also have their own preferences. For many words either way is acceptable, but it is safer to choose 'ise' as this covers a greater number of words.

However, there are certain words that *must* end in 'ize'.

EXAMPLES:

size	prize (when used to mean 'a reward')
capsize	seize

A sound problem

Here we will consider sounds which, at the ends of words, can cause confusion.

▶ final 'k' sound

▶ final 'g' sound

▶ 'ture'

▶ 'ate'

▶ 'ain'

▶ 'age'

▶ 'ion'

A final 'k' sound

ic

EXAMPLES:

frantic	electric	plastic	polytechnic
public	traffic	economic	pneumatic

In order for this hard 'c' sound to be retained, it is necessary to insert 'k' before adding 'ed', 'ing', 'er' or 'y'.

EXAMPLES:

picnic becomes picnicked

mimic becomes mimicking

traffic becomes trafficker

panic becomes panicky

When you want to add 'ly' to words ending in 'ic', you need to add 'al' before the 'ly' ending.

e.g. frantic becomes frantically

Similarly,

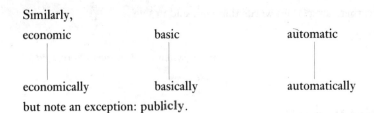

economic   basic   automatic

economically   basically   automatically

but note an exception: **publicly**.

que

Some words of French origin use the letters **que** to make a final 'k' sound.

EXAMPLES:

unique	cheque
antique	technique

A final 'g' sound

▶ In many words the hard 'g' sound at the end of words is naturally made by 'g'.

EXAMPLES:

flag   wag   leg

▶ In other words 'g' combines with 'n'.

EXAMPLES:

sing   flung   prong

▶ A few words have their final 'g' sound made by **gue**.

EXAMPLES:

fatigue   intrigue   colleague   catalogue   Portuguese

The 'u' is silent but essential. Without it the 'g' would make a soft 'g' sound as 'e' would occur after 'g'.

Concentrate on these words as a group so that you can learn to spell them.

'ture'

EXAMPLES:

picture	capture	moisture	departure
future	lecture	mixture	furniture

When you say these words aloud, you may hear a slight 'ch' sound at the beginning of the last syllable. There are not many words with this ending so it is best to learn each as it occurs in your writing.

'ate'

EXAMPLES:

appropriate	alternate	affectionate	obstinate
celebrate	complicate	elaborate	demonstrate
intricate	delicate	accurate	candidate
associate	translate	fluctuate	hibernate

Usually these endings do not cause too many problems as in most words it is possible to hear the **ate** sound at the end. But in some words (e.g. 'affectionate' and 'obstinate') the **ate** ending isn't so clear.

Exaggerate the **ate** ending or pick out the word 'ate' at the end of the word to deal with this group. Read the words aloud and note down those which do not have a clear 'ate' sound at the end so that you can learn any that are difficult for you.

'ain'

EXAMPLES:

<u>certain</u>	contain	complain	explain
<u>Britain</u>	fountain	mountain	ca<u>ptain</u>

In some words the **ain** ending is pronounced more clearly than in others. The **ain** in the underlined words sounds more like 'in' than 'ain'.

Group such words together when you learn them so that you can learn a pattern.

'age'

This is another combination of letters that gets swallowed up at the end of words and is best dealt with by stressing the pronunciation of the word 'age'. Such words have already been mentioned in Chapter 13 under the soft 'c' and 'g' sounds.

EXAMPLES:

garage

passage

image

16

'ion'

This is a difficult sound to spell but it can help if you are aware of the possible sounds such an ending can make.

EXAMPLES:

onion   opinion   companion

In these words the final ion makes a 'yun' sound.

EXAMPLES:

union   champion

Here the ion is divided into two syllables: un/i/on and cham/pi/on. The 'i' makes an ē sound and the 'on' an unstressed 'un' sound.

EXAMPLES:

region   religion

Here the 'g' makes a soft sound as it is followed by 'i' and the final syllable sounds like 'jun'.

If you have difficulty with such words, it is best to divide them into pronounceable parts and exaggerate the pronunciation to fit the spelling pattern.

e.g. dom in i on spells dominion.

General advice for endings

▶ Use the guidelines in this chapter as a reference source so that you can keep returning to check words that you are uncertain about.

▶ Exaggerating the pronunciation of endings is most helpful.

▶ Where there are alternative ways of making the same sound, be aware of the various possibilities, then try each letter combination and see which looks right.

▶ Always use a dictionary as your final check; it is easy to find the word you want as you already know how to spell a substantial part of the word.

As you use and write the words contained in this chapter, you will become familiar with their patterns and will feel more confident about spelling them.

17
Prefixes

What is a prefix?

A prefix is a group of letters added at the beginning of a word.

e.g. untrue

A prefix changes the meaning of a word.

e.g. True means genuine; untrue means false.

Prefixes can have Greek, Latin or Old English origins.

A prefix is a group of letters added at the beginning of a word to change the meaning of the word.

Why is it useful to know about prefixes?

Prefixes help with spelling. You will be more successful at dividing words into syllables if you can recognise them. By combining your knowledge of prefixes and suffixes, you will find it easier to build up and spell long words. Knowing the meaning of a prefix can also help you work out the meaning of an unfamiliar word.

The prefix rule

Adding a prefix to a word is quite straightforward.

▶ A word does not change its spelling when a prefix is added.
▶ The spelling of a prefix usually remains constant.
▶ A prefix ending in a vowel never changes its spelling.
▶ A prefix ending in a consonant only changes its spelling in a few situations.

Section 3

17

A spelling guide

dis	un	in
dissimilar	unnerve	innumerable
dissatisfied	unnecessary	innocuous

ir	im	il
irrelevant	immature	illegal
irregular	immoral	illogical

	mis	
	misspell	
	misspent	

In all these words the prefix ends with the same letter as the word begins. The prefix doesn't alter. The word doesn't alter. Knowing how the prefix is spelt can help you decide how to spell a word. Take special note of this spelling guide as it will help you with tricky words.

Testing the spelling guide

** Choose the word within each pair which is spelt correctly. Remember the prefixes are spelt dis, un, in, ir, im, mis and il.

disappear/dissappear   disolve/dissolve

illegible/ilegible   irresponsible/iresponsible

imeasurable/immeasurable inumerate/innumerate

unatural/unnatural   immobolise/imobilise

misshapen/mishapen   irelegious/irreligious

Simple prefixes

over   up   under   out   all   well

These prefixes are easy to deal with as they are everyday words whose meanings are well known.

In the diagrams opposite you will notice that there can be changes to the prefix when **all** and **well** are added to words. You have already read about this in Chapter 6.

When the prefix **all** is added to a word, one 'l' is always dropped. In all hyphenated words, **well** remains unchanged but in 'welcome' and 'welfare' one 'l' is dropped.

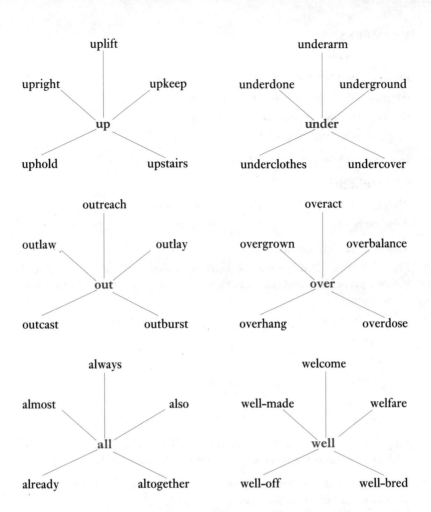

uplift
upright · up · upkeep
uphold · upstairs

underarm
underdone · under · underground
underclothes · undercover

outreach
outlaw · out · outlay
outcast · outburst

overact
overgrown · over · overbalance
overhang · overdose

always
almost · all · also
already · altogether

welcome
well-made · well · welfare
well-off · well-bred

Direct opposites

When certain prefixes are added to words they reverse the meaning of the word.

e.g. **un**happy

| un | il | im | in | ir |

All of the above prefixes mean 'not'.

EXAMPLES:

unarmed means not armed

ineligible means not eligible

irreplaceable means not able to be replaced

imperfect means not perfect

illegitimate means not lawful

In some words dis also means 'not'.

EXAMPLES:

disapprove	discontinue
disadvantageous	disobey

Making the right choice

Problems arise when it comes to knowing which prefix should be placed before a particular word. This can only be decided by listening to the *sound* of the word.

e.g. Which sounds right?

    unpolite

    inpolite

    irpolite

    impolite

    ilpolite

'Impolite' is correct, but the choice between 'inpolite' and 'impolite' can be difficult as in speech it is not easy to hear which prefix has been used.

Remember the prefix 'in' is never used before 'p' or 'm'; 'im' is always used before these letters.

EXAMPLES:

improbable	impersonal
immigrant	immortal

** Use the correct prefix ('un', 'in', 'ir', 'im', 'il' or 'dis') to form the complete opposite of each of these words.

dependent	believe	patient	audible
liberal	offensive	recoverable	manageable
orderly	certain	rational	modest

Using prefixes for meaning

If you know the meaning of a prefix, it can help you to work out the meaning of a word.

** Work out the meaning of these prefixes from the words in the list beside each of them.

re		sur	
	regain		surcharge
	reword		surpass
	return		surplus
	recapture		surtax
	refresh		surface
	reunion		surmount

inter		trans	
	international		transplant
	interchange		transact
	interwoven		transatlantic
	intercontinental		transcontinental
	interdepartmental		transit
	interlock		transfix

super		mis	
	superabundance		misdeed
	superfine		misspell
	superhuman		miscalculate
	superman		mislead
	supernatural		misused
	supertanker		misfortune

17

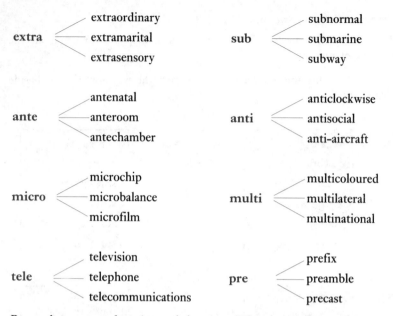

extra — extraordinary / extramarital / extrasensory	**sub** — subnormal / submarine / subway
ante — antenatal / anteroom / antechamber	**anti** — anticlockwise / antisocial / anti–aircraft
micro — microchip / microbalance / microfilm	**multi** — multicoloured / multilateral / multinational
tele — television / telephone / telecommunications	**pre** — prefix / preamble / precast

Remember **ante** and **anti** sound the same. When you want to spell a word beginning with one of these prefixes, think about its meaning and then you won't spell the word incorrectly.

Size or number

demi means half

semi means half

hemi means half

hyper means too much

hypo means too little or inadequate

mono means single

bi means twice or double

tri means threefold

mega means large

centi means one hundredth

** The prefixes above all denote size or number. Work out the meaning of each word below from its prefix; use a dictionary to check your definitions.

demigod	semicolon	hemisphere
hyperactive	biannual	hypothermia
bilingual	centilitre	trident
monotone	trimester	megalomania

Less common prefixes

** Find at least one word which begins with each prefix covered so far. Check that the word you have chosen exactly fits the meaning of the prefix. Use your dictionary for these further examples.

pseudo means false

circum means round or around

ultra means extreme or beyond

arch means chief

photo means light

homo means same

omni means all

auto means self

Word building

By identifying and understanding prefixes and suffixes, you have a far greater control over words and their spellings.

** Remove the prefixes and suffixes from these words so that you end up with the base words. In some cases you may need to adjust the spelling of the final base word as, although the spelling of a word does not change when a prefix is added, it can change when a suffix is added.

discreditable

uneasily

disgraceful

refreshment

miscalculation

unserviceable

impoliteness

misbehaviour

imperfection

dissatisfaction

inharmonious

misquoting

unsteadily

unfortunately

replacement

impatiently

immovable

misapplication

unnecessarily

disappearance

17

18
Dealing with Doubt

He should, of course, have asked for insulating tape! At some time or another most of us have made similar mistakes. While situations like this can be funny, many of us don't like to appear foolish – particularly if we are in a formal situation. On these occasions the right choice of word and the correct spelling is very important. If we have doubts about either of these, it can inhibit our writing and damage our confidence.

This chapter looks at many of those words which can create doubt and uncertainty for the writer.

Common confusions

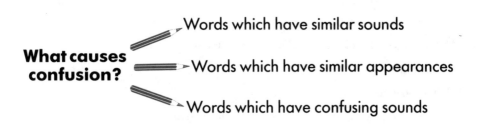

What causes confusion?
- Words which have similar sounds
- Words which have similar appearances
- Words which have confusing sounds

Words which have similar sounds

In Chapter 15 you were given many examples of homophones (pairs of words with exactly the same sound but a different spelling and meaning). There are, however, other pairs or groups of words which can be confused because they have a similar sound.

- of and off
- we're, were, where and wear
- quiet and quite
- affect and effect
- addition and edition

of and off
EXAMPLES:

He asked for a pound of tomatoes.

He rode off without saying goodbye.

Helpful Hints

▶ Listen carefully when you read the sentences: 'of' sounds like 'ov'; 'off' has a distinct 'f' sound.

▶ Don't confuse 'of' with 'have'. They can sound similar and so 'of' is frequently used incorrectly when 'have' is required.

EXAMPLES:

He must **have** come back. ✔

He must **of** come back. ✗

▶ Remember, 'of' shows a connection or relationship, or a sense of belonging.

Section 3

18

EXAMPLES:

a pound of tomatoes

a director of a company

** Use either 'of', 'off' or 'have' in each of these sentences.

1 She can't .... heard.

2 The book fell .... the shelf.

3 There were hundreds .... people at the match.

4 They will .... gone home by now.

5 They sang four verses .... the song.

6 The team walked .... the pitch.

7 He isn't one .... the nicest people in the world.

8 I must .... fallen asleep.

we're, were, where and wear

▶ we're is the shortened form of 'we are'.

e.g. We're going home.

▶ were is a verb or part of verb.

e.g. They were running.

▶ where is a 'place' word.

e.g. Where is it?

▶ wear is a verb meaning 'to be dressed in'.

e.g. We wear clothes.

Helpful Hints

▶ Listen to the difference in sound between the words. Only 'where' and 'wear' have exactly the same sound.

▶ Remember the meaning and spelling of 'where' by learning the mnemonic:

here, there and everywhere.

▶ Use this sentence to help you with 'wear':

we wear earrings and rings.

quiet and quite

▶ quiet means undisturbed.

e.g. The empty room was **quiet** and peaceful.

▶ quite means completely.

e.g. It was **quite** full.

Remember the difference by the sentence:

A qui et secr et is whispered.

or by dividing 'quiet' into two parts (qui/et) and then exaggerating the final 'et'.

affect and effect

▶ affect is a verb meaning to change, alter or influence.

e.g. Acid rain affected the trees.

▶ effect is a noun meaning the result of an action.

e.g. The effect of his accident is still apparent.

Helpful Hints

▶ **Affect** can mean to alter; remember a for alter.

▶ Exaggerate the pronunciation (affect or effect) when you see either of them in print so you appreciate their individual meanings. When you write the words, stress the ă or ē at the beginning.

▶ 'Effect' is very occasionally used as a verb – meaning to carry out or bring about.

e.g. The army effected a swift retreat.

addition and edition

addition   edition

a thing added   one of a series of books, magazines or programmes

Learn the mnemonics:

An editor edits an edition.

An addition is added.

Words which have similar appearances

Some words may look similar but are actually pronounced quite differently. If you have difficulty with any of these pairs, check the meaning of the words in a dictionary and then try to remember them by exaggerating the pronunciation even more.

** Complete each sentence with the correct word from the pair.

1 It was .... than he thought. (later/latter)

2 Of the two, Karl preferred the .... (later/latter)

3 I .... your remark. (recent/resent)

4 It is the most .... edition. (recent/resent)

5 He will .... the position. (accept/except)

6 All the crew were ready, ... the captain. (accept/except)

7 The road went .... a series of tunnels. (through/thorough)

8 A .... search was made. (through/thorough)

9 The .... manager was at the interview. (personnel/personal)

10 Your .... life is your own affair. (personnel/personal)

Words which have confusing sounds

choose and chose

choose has an 'oo' sound and rhymes with 'snooze'.

chose has an ō sound and rhymes with 'doze'.

You could remember the difference between these by the sentence

I choose to snooze, but he chose to doze.

loose and lose

The vowel sound in both of these verbs is the same – an 'oo' sound. However, the 's' in 'loose' sounds like 's', while the 's' in 'lose' sounds like 'z'.

You could remember 'loose' by the phrase

a loose tooth (each has 'oo').

Or you could try to remember 'lose' by linking it mentally with 'lost'.

If you lose your money, it is lost.

the silent 'e' effect

Compare these two lists.

breath	breathe
cloth	clothe
bath	bathe
human	humane
moral	morale

In Chapter 9 you were shown the 'vowel–consonant-e' pattern. The words in these two lists sometimes cause the writer to doubt whether the right choice has been made. However, by remembering the silent 'e' effect (which makes the vowel before it long), it is easier to distinguish the words within their pairs.

EXAMPLES:

breath (ĕ)	breathe (ē)
moral (ă)	morale (ā)

Notice also the effect on the 'l' in 'morale' – the word sounds like 'morarl'.

e.g. The army's morale was high before the battle.

'all' words

What are the differences in meaning between these pairs of words?

all ready	already
all together	altogether
all ways	always

all ready means all of them were ready.

e.g. They were all ready to leave. (every person)

already means previously.

e.g. He had already left when she 'phoned.

all together means all in a group.

e.g. Their cases were all together on the platform.

altogether means completely.

e.g. Altogether, they raised £1000 for OXFAM.

all ways means all of the ways.

e.g. He tried all ways of opening it.

always means every time.

e.g. I always eat breakfast.

all right means everything correct.

e.g. The results of his experiments were all right.

all right also means fine.

e.g. 'I'm all right, thank you.'

Although you may see 'alright' meaning 'fine' written as one word, it is not considered good English. *Always* use 'all right' as two separate words.

'ed' or 't'

Throughout this book we have used the word 'spelt'; this could have been written 'spelled'.

A few verbs can have an 'ed' or 't' ending in the past tense.

verb	past tense
spoil	spoiled or spoilt
burn	burned or burnt
kneel	kneeled or knelt
learn	learned or learnt
dream	dreamed or dreamt
spill	spilled or spilt (one 'l')
spell	spelled or spelt (one 'l')

If you forget which verbs can be spelt either way, then *always* use the 'ed' ending and you'll *always* be right.

Acceptable alternative spellings

Although you might find certain dictionaries prefer one of the spellings in each of these pairs, it is generally accepted that either is correct.

despatch	dispatch
enquire	inquire
farther	further (when referring to distance)

e.g. How much further/farther is there to go?

gaol	jail
curb	kerb (when referring to pavement or paving stones)

e.g. The damaged curb/kerb stones were replaced.

Same spelling – different stress

Look at these two sentences.

The refuse was collected every Monday.

I refuse to marry you.

In the first sentence, the stress falls on the first part of the word refuse; in the second it falls on the second syllable, refuse. Notice that the spelling stays the same but changing the stress makes it sound as though two different spellings are being used.

Listen to the way the stress pattern changes in the word 'permit' in these sentences.

He will permit you to leave.

You must apply for a permit.

** Using a dictionary, find the differences in meaning between these pairs of words.

desert	invalid	minute	perfect
desert	invalid	minute	perfect

Same spelling – different pronunciation

These one-syllable words can be pronounced in two ways, each of which has a different meaning.

row (ō) means to propel with oars, or a line or rank of people or things.

row ('ouch' sound) means a noisy squabble.

** Give the meanings of the two pronunciations of each of these pairs of words.

bow ('ouch' sound) and bow (ō)

sow ('ouch' sound) and sow (ō)

lead (ē) and lead (ĕ)

read (ē) and read (ĕ)

tear (rhymes with 'air') and tear (rhymes with 'ear')

wind (ĭ) and wind (ī)

live (ī) and live (ĭ)

Removing the doubt

** Find the word from each pair that matches the clue. You might need to check your ideas in a dictionary.

e.g. eligible

    illegible   writing which is difficult to read

illegible is the correct answer.

1 elicit
  illicit   unlawful

2 eminent
  imminent   famous or distinguished

3 emigrant
  immigrant   a person who comes into a country

4 formerly
  formally   previously

5 procrastinate
  prevaricate   delay starting

6 aural
  oral   to do with hearing

7 liable
  libel   likely to

8 intelligible
  intelligent   easily understood

9 insure
  ensure   make certain of

10 septic
   sceptic   full of bacteria

One letter or two?

Is it 'innoculate', 'inocculate', 'innocculate' or 'inoculate'?

inoculate

one needle   one cry

Is it 'harass' 'harrass' 'haras' or 'harras'?

harass

Rita sued Simon for harassing her.

Double letters often cause doubt.

Remember the techniques:

    visualising the word

    syllabification

    adapting the pronunciation

    mnemonics

** Choose the correct spelling in each pair of words below. If you are uncertain, or if when you check the answers you find you have made the wrong choice, find a technique to help you learn the correct spelling.

vacinate/vaccinate	inflamable/inflammable
dessicated/desiccated	woolen/woollen
parallel/paralell	bazar/bazaar
aleviate/alleviate	colossal/collossal
immense/imense	opponent/oponent
assassin/asassin	abreviate/abbreviate

Difficult numbers

Learning words within their groups will help you to appreciate the family pattern and to spell difficult number words with confidence.

18

Can you see a pattern in the following groups of words?

four	fourth
fourteen	fourteenth
forty	fortieth

eight	eighth
eighteen	eighteenth
eighty	eightieth

nine	ninth
nineteen	nineteenth
ninety	ninetieth

What's the silent letter?

You have already been shown several examples of silent letters in Chapters 5 and 8.

** Identify the silent letter or letters in each of these words. When you have done this, see if you can find any patterns for when a particular letter can be silent. Select any words from the list that may be useful to you and think of techniques for remembering how to spell them.

reminiscent	conscience	exhilarated
rhetoric	crescent	obsolescent
jeopardise	rhubarb	fluorescent
catarrh	adjudicator	psychology
repertory	adjacent	environment
dinghy	effervescent	knapsack
rheumatism	chronicle	rhinoceros
bronchitis	transcend	pneumatic

As you write and develop your spelling, you will encounter more words containing silent letters. It will help if you list them so that you become aware of what silent letters there are, what they can do to words and how they appear in certain word groups.

Final thoughts

By now you should be aware of the many ways English spelling does conform to rules or sound patterns. Think about the section you have just read.

▶ Do you need to return to a particular chapter to refresh your knowledge?

▶ Did you find any rules or patterns especially difficult? If so, can you find other ways of coping with these words?

▶ Which group or groups of words do you need to spend more time learning?

▶ Think of ways you can build on the practice you have already been given in this section.

18

Over to You

By now you will have practised the various techniques for learning words and will have a sound knowledge of the main rules and spelling patterns. Spelling should no longer be a mystery to you as you are aware of the various letter combinations possible and know what is probable.

As you have worked through the chapters, you will have seen an improvement in your spelling and gained a more confident approach so where do you go from here?

Where do you go from here?

- Analyse words as you come across them.
- Use the techniques outlined in this book.
- Use this book as a reference source.
- Develop the writing habit.
- Increase your wordpower.
- Practise your spelling on a regular basis.
- Build up your own tools.
- Check your writing.
- Have faith in your ability to spell.

Analyse words as you come across them

You have already started to analyse words and examine beginnings, middles, endings and syllables. Build upon this so that you develop an analytical approach to all the words you meet. You have looked at the various reasons why English spelling causes difficulties. Remember these problem areas and train yourself to identify them.

Different combinations of letters can make the same sound

EXAMPLES:

An or sound is made by different combinations of letters in these words: scrawny, tournament, fortune, autumn, and ought.

And an s sound is made by these highlighted letter combinations: soap, scientific, recess and civic.

The same combination of letters can make different sounds
EXAMPLES:

ch makes different sounds in each of the following words: Christmas, chivalry, chaos and cheque.

ai sounds different in each of these words: said, plaid, plain, fair and Britain.

One letter can sound like another letter
EXAMPLES:

c can sound like s (simplicity, implicit).

g can sound like j (congeal, marginal).

a can sound like ĕ (any, many).

o can sound like ŭ (frontier, mongrel).

i can sound like ē (guardian, media).

e can sound like ĭ (pretty, courtesy).

y can sound like ē (clarity, certainty) or ī (comply, rely).

Letters can be silent
EXAMPLES:

bizarre, adjustment, guardian, inexhaustible and honourable.

Double letters

Many people cite double letters as being one of the main obstacles .in spelling. In some words the sounds of the two letters can be heard; others may need to be exaggerated!

EXAMPLES:

assurance	satellite	attached
oppression	compelled	deterrent
assassinate	commemorate	exaggerate
appalling	disappointment	applause

Endings tail off

EXAMPLES:

despondent	temporary
competence	exposure

Beginnings aren't clear

EXAMPLES:

occur	elope	oven
aisle	despise	despite
destruction	destroy	aerial

Homophones

Words can sound the same but be spelt differently according to the way they are used in sentences.

EXAMPLES:

martial and marshal

review and revue

stake and steak

Letters influence other letters within words

e.g. **q(u)** and **w** can change the sound of the vowel that occurs after them.

EXAMPLES:

squash	warrior
squirm	warehouse
quality	woman
quarry	world

Use the techniques outlined in this book

Good spelling largely depends on a good visual memory. All words can be learnt by the visual approach and it should be worked on and developed. However, some people find it quite difficult to picture a word in their minds and then recall this visual image in writing, so they have to resort to other techniques.

Never try to spell a word without first selecting a technique to help you; remember sometimes it is necessary to combine different techniques. If one approach doesn't work, try another. The right techniques are the ones which work for you and the particular word you are trying to learn.

Use this book as a reference source

It isn't possible to remember everything we read and it is often necessary to go back and refresh our memories. We have deliberately repeated certain advice and guidelines throughout this book as we know from experience that students of spelling need more than one reminder.

Use this book as a reference source so that by repeatedly going over problem areas and practising them, your spelling will improve.

Develop the writing habit

Spelling is only one part of good writing, albeit a very important aspect, but don't over emphasise its importance as, ironically, it can make learning to spell more difficult. Aim to improve your spelling as part of the development of your writing as a whole.

Find more reasons to write, write more and be more adventurous in your writing. In that way you will have cause to spell a greater variety of words.

Increase your wordpower

Develop an enthusiasm for words and be curious about them. Try out new words. This book doesn't cover all there is to know about spelling so try to find out more. Read widely and collect words so that you can examine their structures, find ways of committing them to memory and use them.

There is more advice about developing your wordpower in the book about vocabulary in this *Getting to Grips* series.

Practise your spelling on a regular basis

By now you will have realised that spelling isn't a skill you can develop quickly and effortlessly. If you have spelt certain words incorrectly you will have to unlearn those patterns first before you can learn the correct ones. Habits are difficult to break and much practice is needed to acquire new ones.

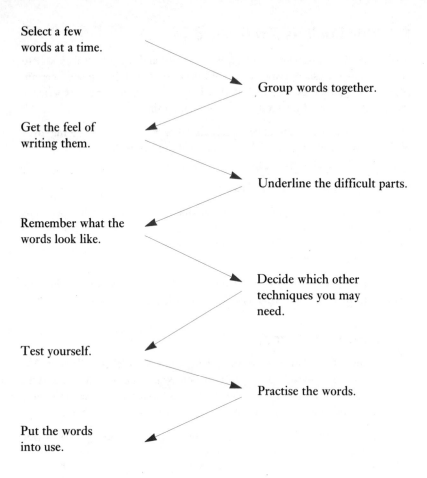

Select a few
words at a time.

Group words together.

Get the feel of
writing them.

Underline the difficult parts.

Remember what the
words look like.

Decide which other
techniques you may
need.

Test yourself.

Practise the words.

Put the words
into use.

Remember: you learn a skill by practising it.

Build up your own tools

Learning to spell is an active endeavour so build up your own bank of
reference sources. This should include

at least one dictionary

a personal word book

personal lists of rules

your own collection of mnemonics, homophones, etc.

Check your writing

Poor spelling can let us down so make certain that anything you write for others is checked thoroughly. We all make mistakes as we write and we all need to check our work. Whenever possible, write a rough draft as this enables you to get your ideas down on paper quickly. When you read your work through and improve upon it, always have a separate check for spelling. During this first spelling-check you will notice words that look wrong but some mistakes may be missed so a second, more critical check is advisable. You are aware of the possible spelling pitfalls so look specifically for these. Your knowledge of the language will allow you to make a more productive check.

Have faith in your ability to spell

You are aware of ways of overcoming your spelling problems, and now have a greater understanding and appreciation of spelling patterns and rules, so feel confident and put this knowledge to good use. You know your shortcomings and you have improved as you've worked through the book, so be patient with yourself and you *will* master spelling.

Understanding the terms

Whilst we have tried to make this book as jargon-free as possible, here is a list of words and terms that may need explanation.

phonemes, the sound patterns that make up the words of a language.

vowels, the letters a, e, i, o and u.

consonants, the remaining 21 letters of the alphabet. The letter 'y' can be described as half vowel and half consonant: in words like 'why' and 'dry' it sounds like an i, but in words like 'yawn' and 'yard' it has a consonant sound.

a short vowel, (shown by a breve (˘) symbol) occurs when a single vowel makes a short sound.

EXAMPLES:

ă in măd

ĕ in tĕn

ĭ in wĭndow

ŏ in lŏst

ŭ in hŭmble

a long vowel, (shown by a macron (¯) symbol) occurs when a single vowel makes a long sound, the same sound as its name.

EXAMPLES:

ā in māte

ē in compēte

ī in fīne

ō in clōthe

ū in cūbe

upper case, capital letters.

e.g.   S   M   FANTASTIC

lower case, not capital letters.

e.g. harbour

consonant blend, two or three consonants which blend together but retain their individual sounds.

EXAMPLES:

'br' in words like brush and brag

'scr' in words like scrape and scratch

'st' in words like list and stop

consonant digraph, two consonants which merge to create a single sound in which neither individual sound is heard.

EXAMPLES:

'wh' in words like wheel and when

'ph' in words like telephone and phonic

syllable, a word or a part of a word that can be made by one effort of breath.

EXAMPLES:

drink has one syllable

paper has two syllables (pa/per)

refreshment has three syllables (re/fresh/ment)

A syllable always contains a vowel or a 'y'.

closed syllable, a syllable which ends in one or more consonants. The vowel in such a syllable usually has a short sound.

EXAMPLES:

open syllable, a syllable ending in a vowel. In such a syllable, the vowel will have a long sound.

EXAMPLES:

singular, one item.

plural, more than one item.

compound word, a word made up of two or more individual words.
e.g. blackberries (black + berries)

base word, a word, complete in itself, which can have a prefix or suffix added to it.

e.g.

re/cover/ing

prefix   base word   suffix

prefix, a syllable or syllables added to the beginning of a word to alter the meaning of the word.

EXAMPLES:

dis satisfied

un known

il legal

suffix, a syllable or syllables added to the end of a word.

EXAMPLES:

walking

fulfilment

vowel suffix, a suffix which begins with a vowel.

EXAMPLES:

skating

laughable

consonant suffix, a suffix which begins with a consonant.

EXAMPLES:

lonely

amendment

homophone, a word that sounds the same as another but has a different spelling and meaning.

EXAMPLES:

meet and meat

some and sum

inflexions, word variants which signal a change in the tense, person, gender, number or case of a word.

e.g. walk, walking, walked, walks.

stress, the part of a word which is emphasised.

EXAMPLES:

media

imperfect

implied

soft c, a 'c' which makes an 's' sound.

e.g. civilise

soft g, a 'g' which makes a 'j' sound.

e.g. gigantic

noun, a naming word: a noun can be the name of a thing, a person, a place, an animal, a quality, an emotion or an idea.

EXAMPLES:

pencil	Ian	honesty
Birmingham	elephant	socialism

verb, a word of action or of state.

EXAMPLES:

to skip

to be

adjective, a word which describes or gives more information about a noun.

EXAMPLES:

yellow paint	final chance	four flowers
adjective noun	adjective noun	adjective noun

Answers

NB No answers are given where you are asked to research words in a dictionary or thesaurus, where answers depend upon personal responses, or where a number of alternative answers is possible.

Chapter 3   Looking at Words

Phonic alternatives

conceal	poison
announce	value
design	parent
scandal	drowsy
forty	recede
procedure	rehearse

Practising

suggestion	straight	thorough
necessary	obey	experience
occasion	building	enthusiastic
really	succeed	muscle
punctual	dissatisfy	people
Tuesday	beautiful	laughter
message	anxious	height
capable	although	early
liaison	bachelor	adjacent

Proof-reading

```
                                    High School
                                    Glenview Road
                                    Blankton
                                    Greyshire
                                    14 February 1992

Mr A. Johnson

36 Stone Lane

Blankton

Greyshire


Dear Mr Johnson,

        I am sorry to have to inform you that your
son, John, has been late for school on three occasions
recently.

        He used to be a very hard-working,
conscientious young man but, since Christmas, he has been
most unreliable and awkward.

        I would be grateful if you could make an
appointment to see me so that we can discuss his
behaviour. Tuesday is the most convenient day for me. My
secretary will make all the necessary arrangements.

        I look forward to meeting you.

        Yours sincerely,



                                Bob Pritchard
```

suppose	succeed	pretty
very	many	only
orange	sign	juice
biscuit	group	queue
mouldy	double	science
weather	disappoint	through

Chapter 4   Taking Words Apart

Helpful hints

1 5 syllables (pro/nun/ci/a/tion)

2 1 syllable (ice)

3 3 syllables (re/mem/ber)

4 2 syllables (but/ter)

5 4 syllables (dis/con/nect/ing)

Practising the technique

Suggested divisions

re/in/force

draw/ing

re/hab/il/it/a/tion

ab/so/lute

or/bit

for/got/ten

car/dig/an

oc/cu/py

un/fit

su/per/vise

Words within words

sup and pose

mate

quaint and acquaint

fright, ten and right

gust, disgust and sting

frost

age and rage

bless, less and sing

or and din

pig and on

Compound words

birdcage

snowball

anything

overlap

chopsticks

cardboard

downstairs

grapefruit

cloakroom

thunderstorm

Reviewing syllables

crim<u>son</u> understand

af<u>ter</u>noon blan<u>ket</u>

pic<u>nic</u> <u>o</u>bey

beg<u>in</u>ning mush<u>room</u>

in<u>ter</u>esting pros<u>per</u>ous

Chapter 5   Adapting the Pronunciation

Consonant digraphs

<u>ch</u>urch <u>ph</u>easant

<u>wh</u>isper <u>th</u>irst

<u>wh</u>isky lur<u>ch</u>

hu<u>sh</u> pa<u>th</u>

<u>sh</u>ake paragra<u>ph</u>

Vowel sounds

defuse (long)	dentist (short)	pupil (long)	acorn (long)
collect (short)	doctor (short)	stake (long)	silent (short)
beware (long)	pistol (short)	saddle (short)	torpedo (long)
hungry (short)	total (long)	hiker (long)	tube (long)
mistake (short)	cabbage (short)	trifle (long)	puppy (short)

Missing syllables

math<u>e</u>matics veg<u>e</u>table

mini<u>a</u>ture lib<u>ra</u>ry

temp<u>e</u>rature virtu<u>all</u>y

serg<u>ea</u>nt vac<u>uu</u>m

parli<u>a</u>ment pe<u>o</u>ple

a<u>c</u>quire Ar<u>c</u>tic

gen<u>e</u>ral monast<u>e</u>ry

Parts of words

convenïent – stress 'ven'   prĕtty – stress ĕ

     – stress ï sound   apparatus – stress 'par'

     – stress 'ent' ending   ĕnemy – stress ĕ

benĕfit – stress ĕ sound   – stress 'my' ending

probably – stress 'bab' syllable

Silent letters

doubt	psalm	descend	mistletoe
kitchen	rhyme	condemn	porridge
ghost	knack	while	bristle
gnaw	love	guitar	edge
knee	known	what	wrinkled

Chapter 6   Knowing the Rules

Testing the rules

quadrangle	college
quirk	cabbage
quake	bandage
quilt	dove
queue	above
cheque	serve
rely	colourful
reply	plentiful
try	forgetful
nudge	almighty
badge	almost

'qu' words	'j' sound ending	'v' sound ending
questionnaire	hedge	twelve
quarantine	plunge	curve
quell	pledge	reserve
picturesque	judge	deprive
squabble	change	attractive
	wage	

ful	fully	'i' sound ending
spiteful	thankfully	try
useful	thoughtfully	fly
pocketful	painfully	cry
masterful		
sinful		

Chapter 7   Using Dictionaries

Dictionary practice

dung<u>eo</u>n	rei<u>m</u>burse	fl<u>u</u>orescent
piti<u>f</u>ul	capsi<u>z</u>e	correspond<u>e</u>nce
effi<u>ci</u>ent	suspi<u>ci</u>ous	paral<u>le</u>l
duplicat<u>o</u>r	misc<u>e</u>llan<u>eo</u>us	ext<u>ra</u>vagant
surv<u>ei</u>llance	dimen<u>si</u>on	depend<u>a</u>ble

Plurals

buffaloes	synopses
indexes/indices	oases
salmon	memorandums/memoranda
cactuses/cacti	criteria
phenomena	gateaus/gateaux

Chapter 8   Jogging the Memory

Collocations

Suggestions:

horrible/terrible	double/trouble	furious/curious
weight/height	disturb/perturb	damage/manage

Anagrams

when	calm	does	during
tongue	height	coupon	people
double	cousin	anxious	brochure
guarantee	ache	punctual	bachelor
opposite	surprise	value	definite

Chapter 9   Short and Long Vowels

When are vowels short?

word	syllables	syllable containing underlined vowel	consonant/s closing that syllable
balance	bal/ance	bal	l
tax	tax	tax	x
pencil	pen/cil	pen	n
tell	tell	tell	ll
omit	o/mit	mit	t
winner	win/ner	win	n
object	ob/ject	ob	b
gossip	gos/sip	gos	s
until	un/til	un	n
sunny	sun/ny	sun	n

ck or k

The interviewer spoke to a number of people who were stricken with grief when they heard of the disaster. Various people put their hands in their pockets and insisted on making a donation to the fund. Several charities said they would put together a package of aid which would include: trucks, blankets and food packets. The shocking news affected the stock market, where dealers started to sell recklessly and share prices suffered a setback.

Two vowels combining to make a short vowel sound

wealthy	spread	steady
pleasure	deafen	heavy
jealous	threaten	already
feather	dreadful	weapon

'vowel–consonant–e' syllables

obsolete	desperate	sincere
amuse	compare/compere	consume
senile	contribute	severe
concise	despite	escape
concrete	promote	scheme
survive	confuse	introduce

ē – 'ee' and 'ea'

appeal	decreasing	exceed
disagreeable	feature	guarantee
proceed	repeated	revealing
succeeded	treaty	breathe

Chapter 10 Same Sound, Different Spelling

'oi' and 'oy'

avoid	annoy	alloy
oil	poise	hoist
employ	exploit	ointment
destroy	choice	appoint
cloy	embroider	invoice
moist	joint	enjoy

'or', 'au', 'aw'

fraud

gauze

audible

audience

auditor

caution

auction

authority

applause

audacious

haulage

'ur', 'ir', 'er' and 'ear'

thirst	swerve	concern	purpose
surprise	purchase	nerve	disturb
service	search	surgeon	suburb
merge	surname	earnest	survive
urgent	member	early	better
circle	furniture	suffer	skirt

Chapter 11   How to Form Plurals

'Hiss' at the end

gases	choruses	benches	arches
witnesses	crosses	hoaxes	fezes
ashes	sixes	bosses	peaches
boxes	larynxes	mattresses	crashes
stitches	stresses		coaches
Christmases	latches		buzzes
			taxes

'y' at the end

ies	**s**
centuries	delays
activities	valleys
opportunities	turkeys
replies	chimneys
factories	monkeys
dictionaries	alloys
flies	donkeys
anxieties	relays

Combining the guidelines

singular	plural	singular	plural
bye-law	bye-laws	circus	circuses
tweezers	tweezers	oasis	oases
blush	blushes	guy	guys
axis	axes	hippopotamus	hippopotami
louse	lice	brooch	brooches
canary	canaries	mouse trap	mouse traps
tattoo	tattoos	lens	lenses
potato	potatoes	ditch	ditches
leaf	leaves	colliery	collieries
wife	wives	beach	beaches
thief	thieves	corridor	corridors
story	stories	gangway	gangways
scientist	scientists	storey	storeys
tidings	tidings	discovery	discoveries
byway	byways	tongs	tongs
pocketful	pocketfuls	criterion	criteria
igloo	igloos	currency	currencies
rodeo	rodeos	class	classes

Chapter 12   Adding Endings

The doubling rule

stopped	banking
cleanest	jammed
explaining	slimmest
flatly	gladden
wrapper	dusty
shutting	grinned
funny	scarred
thinner	crispy
swifter	seeing
fretting	planner

drag	sun	fail
big	scrap	gun
mad	dim	swim
sip	bid	blot
risk	step	drop
flip	hard	fast

The silent 'e' rule

arrival		careless
arriving		caring
arrived		careful
	excitable	
	exciting	
	excited	
requirement		shady
required		shading
requiring		shaded
	useful	
	using	
	useless	
examining		wasteful
examination		wasted
examined		wasting

'y' to 'i' rule

base word	add ing	add er
destroy	destroying	destroyer
tidy	tidying	tidier
worry	worrying	worrier
copy	copying	copier
convey	conveying	conveyer (or conveyor)
buy	buying	buyer
steady	steadying	steadier

base word	add **ly**	add **est**
noisy	noisily	noisiest
lazy	lazily	laziest
easy	easily	easiest
ready	readily	readiest
crazy	crazily	craziest
happy	happily	happiest
base word	add **ed**	add **es**
multiply	multiplied	multiplies
apply	applied	applies
deny	denied	denies
hurry	hurried	hurries
terrify	terrified	terrifies
accompany	accompanied	accompanies
weary	wearied	wearies

The double-syllable rule

admitted	filtered
beginning	gossiped
benefited	gardener
regretful	piloted
profitable	difference
submitted	riveting
transmitted	fidgeted

Chapter 13   The 'c' and 'g' Sounds

Testing the soft 'c' rule

lucid	cylinder	saviour	precise	conceal
reason	saucer	accept	excellent	palace
council	parcel	concentrate	sausage	surface
currency	necessary	solicitor	emergency	electricity

1 December

2 innocent

3 medicine

4 sincerely

5 conceal

6 decide

7 Pacific

8 recital

9 cinema

10 circus

Problem endings

1 The policeman asked to see the motorist's driving <u>licence</u>.
2 His employer asked him to put his ideas into <u>practice</u>.
3 I cannot drive my car until I <u>license</u> it.
4 The teenage girl always ignored her mother's <u>advice</u>.
5 Every evening Clare had to <u>practise</u> her part in the play.
6 He hoped that his latest <u>device</u> would eventually be manufactured.
7 "I strongly <u>advise</u> you not to enter the competition."
8 I frequently <u>devise</u> ideas for improving efficiency at the office.

Hard and soft 'g'

hard 'g'	soft 'g'
guarantee	gyrate
game	gist
ghost	giraffe
granite	general
gutter	gentry
great	gentle
glaze	genius
	geography
	gesture

Testing the soft 'g' rule

gipsy/gypsy	gymnasium	charge
ginger	hinge	merge
negligent	generation	tragic
oxygen	dredge	pageant
barrage	garage	agency

Crossword

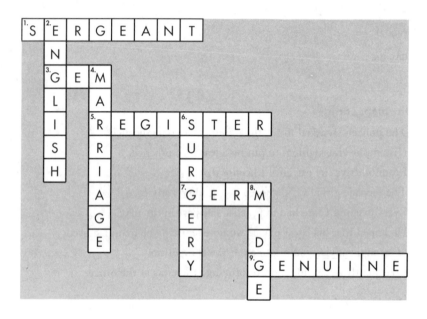

Chapter 14 'i' before 'e'

Testing the 'i' before 'e' rule

diesel	conceive	weight
freight	shriek	perceive
thief	achieve	relief
neighbour	vein	field
brief	deceive	grieve
deceit	besiege	priest
piece	retrieve	chief

Other 'sh' words

torren<u>ti</u>al	spe<u>ci</u>al	spa<u>ci</u>ous
pa<u>ti</u>ent	vi<u>ci</u>ous	infec<u>ti</u>ous
so<u>ci</u>ally	pre<u>ci</u>ous	cons<u>ci</u>ous
deli<u>ci</u>ous	ficti<u>ti</u>ous	finan<u>ci</u>al
opti<u>ci</u>an	appre<u>ci</u>ate	electri<u>ci</u>an

Chapter 15   Informed Choice

Two, to and too

It was <u>too</u> dark <u>to</u> see the buildings which surrounded him but the faint sound of the motorway traffic made him realise that he had gone <u>too</u> far. He had hoped <u>to</u> be near the river. However, it seemed that, although he had been walking for <u>two</u> hours, he wasn't going <u>to</u> reach his destination yet. He was tired, and hungry <u>too</u>. Impatience made him break into a run. He was willing <u>to</u> risk being heard, if he could get <u>to</u> the mooring in time.

its and it's

1 <u>It's</u> been a long time.

2 The company announced an increase in <u>its</u> profits.

3 The cat opened <u>its</u> eyes and stretched.

4 If <u>it's</u> too hot, leave it until it cools down.

5 I don't like to be too inquisitive but <u>it's</u> very puzzling.

6 The shop will be closing <u>its</u> doors in a few minutes.

7 <u>It's</u> no wonder he failed his driving test.

8 He doesn't like the car because <u>it's</u> too small.

9 The roof leaks when <u>it's</u> raining.

10 <u>Its</u> tyres look quite worn.

there, their, and they're

MYRA   There/here is the cinema. I said it was over there/here.

TONY   There is an enormous queue. I think they're all waiting for the film on screen two. I can hear the manager shouting that there are only twenty seats left.

MYRA   Shall we wait here/there/too or go round and see Mike and John?

TONY   We could go round to their house. It's/They're not too far from here and I know they're usually at home on a Thursday evening.

passed and past

1 The car sped past the finish at 150 mph.

2 The car looks past its best.

3 Mrs Redwood passed the message on to the manager.

4 It's past his bedtime.

5 His past career was remarkable.

6 In spite of all their fears, she passed the examination.

7 The house is just past the library.

8 We will forget about the past.

9 The car passed its MOT.

10 She remembered her past mistakes.

Common homophones

miner minor	morning mourning	steal steel
story storey	board bored	grown groan
hall haul	peer pier	pair pear pare
caught court	altar alter	shoot chute
style stile	allowed aloud	hire higher

stair and stare	mind and mined
shore and sure	muscle and mussel
air and heir	lesson and lessen

ceiling and <u>sealing</u>   stayed and st<u>ai</u>d

metal and me<u>ttle</u>   piece and p<u>eace</u>

hour and <u>our</u>   navel and na<u>val</u>

1 A part of a church   <u>aisle</u>

An area of land surrounded by water   <u>isle</u>

2 A vault   <u>cellar</u>

A vendor   <u>seller</u>

3 A discovery   <u>find</u>

Made to pay a penalty   <u>fined</u>

4 Used to measure the value of gold and diamonds   <u>carat</u>

A vegetable   <u>carrot</u>

5 Caused by a burst pipe   <u>leak</u>

Popular with Welsh people   <u>leek</u>

6 Rubbish?   <u>waste</u>

This measurement often causes concern   <u>waist</u>

7 Film or pop star?   <u>idol</u>

Lazy   <u>idle</u>

8 Payment for a journey   <u>fare</u>

Reasonable   <u>fair</u>

9 Smaller than a raisin   <u>currant</u>

Happening now   <u>current</u>

10 To caution someone   <u>warn</u>

Showing the effects of age   <u>worn</u>

More difficult homophones

1 Help me to <u>prise</u> this lid off.

2 He kept a <u>hoard</u> of tinned food in his cupboard.

3 The accused intends to <u>waive</u> his right to speak.

4 There was a <u>sheer</u> drop below them.

5 The mooring rope was pulled <u>taut</u> in the gale.

6 The <u>councillor</u> won the local election.

7 You can claim tax relief if she is your <u>dependant</u>.

8 The teacher had a reputation for being <u>forthright</u>.

9 The race<u>course</u> measured two miles.

10 Most people enjoy receiving a <u>compliment</u> about their appearance.

Chapter 16   Word Endings

Using the guidelines

stab<u>le</u>	dent<u>al</u>	ment<u>al</u>
coast<u>al</u>	responsib<u>le</u>	vegetab<u>le</u>
fat<u>al</u>	terrib<u>le</u>	nav<u>al</u>
scand<u>al</u>	sand<u>al</u>	cryst<u>al</u>
reb<u>el</u>	rust<u>le</u>	sing<u>le</u>

Using the guidelines

His <u>unmistakable</u> ability as a musician is instantly <u>recognisable</u> and it is <u>inevitable</u> that he will eventually become famous. By nature he is <u>sociable,</u> <u>hospitable, excitable, changeable</u> and at times even <u>miserable</u>. The press always remarks upon his <u>fashionable</u> clothes and his <u>terrible</u> temper.

justifiable	inflammable	objectionable	adorable
irritable	reputable	navigable	commendable
applicable	variable	admirable	estimable

Applying the guidelines

<u>ate</u>	<u>ct</u>	<u>it</u>	<u>ession</u>
calculator	instructor	inheritor	possessor
creator	inspector	creditor	
radiator	elector		
dictator			

selector	computer	survivor	inventor
player	conqueror	supervisor	distributor/er
surveyor	deserter	competitor	error
traveller	councillor	fertiliser	customer

Choosing endings

cemet<u>ery</u>	bound<u>ary</u>
surg<u>ery</u>	regist<u>ry</u>
necess<u>ary</u>	custom<u>ary</u>
cook<u>ery</u>	chival<u>ry</u>
infant<u>ry</u>	lavat<u>ory</u>
discov<u>ery</u>	ordin<u>ary</u>
poult<u>ry</u>	myst<u>ery</u>
mem<u>ory</u>	milit<u>ary</u>

tion/sion/ssion

omission	collision	profession	separation	destruction
invention	abolition	competition	decision	confusion
revision	television	infection	composition	explosion

Trying out the guidelines

studious	curious
mysterious	glorious
conscientious	adventurous
gracious	religious
spacious	humorous

Chapter 17   Prefixes

Testing the spelling guide

disappear	dissolve
illegible	irresponsible
immeasurable	innumerate
unnatural	immobilise
misshapen	irreligious

Making the right choice

independent	disbelieve	impatient	inaudible
illiberal	inoffensive	irrecoverable	unmanageable
disorderly	uncertain	irrational	immodest

Using prefixes for meaning

re means again	sur means over/above/beyond
inter means between/among/together	trans means across/through/beyond
super means above/over	mis means badly/wrong
extra means more than necessary	sub means under/below
ante means before	anti means act against/opposed to
micro means extremely small	multi means much/many
tele means far/distant	pre means in front of

Word building

credit	harmony
easy	quote
grace	steady
fresh	fortune
calculate	place
service	patient
polite	move
behave	apply
perfect	necessary
satisfy	appear

Chapter 18   Dealing with Doubt

of, off and have

1 She can't <u>have</u> heard.

2 The book fell <u>off</u> the shelf.

3 There were hundreds <u>of</u> people at the match.

4 They will <u>have</u> gone home by now.

5 They sang four verses <u>of</u> the song.

6 The team walked <u>off</u> the pitch.

7 He isn't one <u>of</u> the nicest people in the world.

8 I must <u>have</u> fallen asleep.

Similar appearance

1 It was <u>later</u> than he thought.

2 Of the two, Karl preferred the <u>latter</u>.

3 I <u>resent</u> your remark.

4 It is the most <u>recent</u> edition.

5 He will <u>accept</u> the position.

6 All the crew were ready, <u>except</u> the captain.

7 The road went <u>through</u> a series of tunnels.

8 A <u>thorough</u> search was made.

9 The <u>personnel</u> manager was at the interview

10 Your <u>personal</u> life is your own affair.

Removing the doubt

1 illicit

2 eminent

3 immigrant

4 formerly

5 procrastinate

6 aural

7 liable

8 intelligible

9 ensure

10 septic

One letter or two?

vaccinate	inflammable
desiccated	woollen
parallel	bazaar
alleviate	colossal
immense	opponent
assassin	abbreviate

What's the silent letter?

reminiscent	conscience	exhilarated
rhetoric	crescent	obsolescent
jeopardise	rhubarb	fluorescent
catarrh	adjudicator	psychology
repertory	adjacent	environment
dinghy	effervescent	knapsack
rheumatism	chronicle	rhinoceros
bronchitis	transcend	pneumatic

Index